THE
SEARCH FOR
AN ETERNAL NORM

As Represented by Three Classics

Louis J. Halle

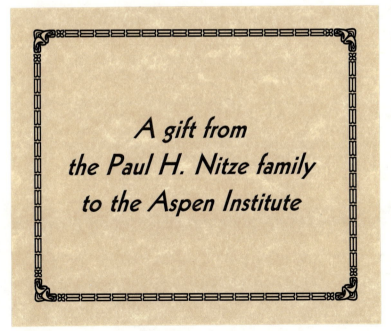

*A gift from
the Paul H. Nitze family
to the Aspen Institute*

UNIVERSITY
PRESS OF
AMERICA

Library of Congress Catalog Card Number: **80-5793**

CONTENTS

Other books by Louis J. Halle

We must not forget that Aristotle . . .
distinguishes tragedy from other forms of
drama not as the form that represents human misery but as that which represents
human goodness or nobleness. . . . The
powers of evil and horror must be granted
their full scope; it is only thus that we
can triumph over them. Only when they
have worked their uttermost will do we
realize that there remains something in
man's soul which is forever beyond their
grasp and has power in its own right to
make life beautiful. This is the great revelation, or the great illusion, of tragedy.

—Gilbert Murray

GENERAL INTRODUCTION

> We're made so that we love
> First when we see them painted,
> things we have passed
> Perhaps a hundred times nor cared to see.
>
> —Browning's _Fra Lippo Lippi_

One of the senses in which the word "philosophy" may be used is suggested by Rousseau's reference to "the philosophy needed by man so that he may know how to observe for once what he has seen every day." As each of us moves about the world our eyes register a multiplicity of images that may be the same for each of us up to the point at which they reach the threshold of our minds. But the ways in which our minds receive them, if they cross the threshold at all, vary widely. For instance, one who has no interest in nature may walk with open eyes through fields where flocks of birds are feeding and, if asked afterwards whether there had been any birds along his way, have to report that he had not noticed any. Another will report that he vaguely recalled having seen some. A third will give a list of species seen, together with an estimate of the numbers of each.

On the basis of the difference between seeing and observing, every mind exercises a largely automatic exclusion made necessary by a mental capacity limited at best. Perhaps all of us have to exclude the mass of raw experiences that come our way in order to reserve our capacity for those that correspond to our disposition, interests, or training. Socrates, in so far as he could, deliberately excluded the whole tangible world because it interfered with his concentration on "ideas," which he regarded as the only reality.

The distinction between seeing and observing warrants a writer in calling attention to what, after the reader observes it, may be recognized as elementary. It is in terms that seem to me elementary that I have dealt with three classics of literature in the pages that follow.

What are these terms ?

Every authentic work of literature, art, or music represents a vision of this realm of being in terms of what it is or what it might be. As such, it is a philosophical vision, so that one can say of Bach's B-minor Mass or Botticelli's Venus or Homer's Odyssey, as of Plato's Republic, Hobbes's Leviathan, and Kant's Critique of Pure Reason, that it is essentially a work of philosophy. Where a philosophy is explicit in Plato, Hobbes, and Kant, it is implicit in the music, the painting, and the poetry.

I am bound, however, to draw a chastening conclusion from the whole libraries of exegesis that have accumulated about each of the classic works of music, art, or literature. It is the conclusion most vividly expressed in the old Jain tale of the blind men and the elephant : what seems self-evident about the elephant's shape to the man who has hold of its tail differs from what seems self-evident to the one who has hold of its ear. My own disposition to see works of art as expressions of philosophy is not generally shared. It follows that, when I set forth what I take to be the basic or elementary content of Hamlet, of The Odyssey, or of Le Morte d'Arthur, a due respect for the observation of others requires that I present it as a personal view, although it seems to me more than that.

One measure of a writer's success is that the points

he makes come to seem obvious to his reader even when they had never occurred to him before. I have therefore allowed myself, on occasion, to take it as a compliment when a critic has complained that I was saying what everyone knew, consoling myself with the thought that I may have caused the critic to observe what he had only seen before. This can be tested, however, by an examination of the literature. A respected and friendly reader of my essay on Hamlet raised the question whether it contained anything new, since so many of its points seemed obvious. I had only to refer him to the vast body of Hamlet criticism; and even on the detailed commentary of Chapter II, where I was free to make points that were commonplace, I could ask him to test the points I made against that compendium of detailed commentary by others, Furness's Variorum edition. At the least, such an examination would show that there was lack of agreement on many of my points, and that there were other points, not a few, which it would be hard or impossible to find at all in the literature. My citations of Dr. J. Dover Wilson in the essay itself illustrate all this.

In the case of my essay on The Odyssey I have cited the interpretations of two critics generally regarded as representing the highest distinction, and of a third who could be taken less seriously if he were not representative. Let the reader go beyond these citations to read as far as he wishes in centuries of accumulated commentary on The Odyssey, he will still find the same sort of thing.

I recognize that literary criticism is validly practiced at a variety of levels, from textual and linguistic analysis, through elucidation by social and cultural historians, to the search for deeper meanings. I have, myself, been concerned only with meaning in the terms that I define below.

+   +   +

What is basic to human life, as distinct from all

3

other life, is a discrepancy between a normative order in men's minds and the existential circumstances in which they actually find themselves. Every human individual must necessarily have in his mind, whether he formulates it or not, and even if he is not conscious of it at all, a conception of some order that is proper in terms of what God or Nature intended. (It makes no difference whether he does or does not believe either in God or in a Nature that has intentions.) To take the simplest example, all of us would agree that our kind properly walk on two limbs where horses properly walk on all four. Saying that "Nature intended" us to walk on two limbs may be merely a figure of speech, yet the normative distinction, the distinction between what is and what is not proper to us, remains.

When it comes to conduct that is not purely instinctive, each of us has to have a normative order in his mind on which to base it. He has no other way of deciding what he ought to do and how he ought to do it.

On many points of normative order, such as the proper mode of walking, all of us from the Hottentot to the Eskimo would agree. But on such matters as ethics and social organization the conflict of views is general and intense. People who believe neither in God nor in a Nature that has intentions, like the French school of existentialists, may nevertheless be passionately committed to the propriety of a certain social order and the impropriety of others.

My own disposition is agnostic. Although I am moved by conceptions of propriety that are not without foundation in what present themselves to me as religious insights, I find no reason to believe that there is one preordained normative order to which we men should conform our social relations, including the organization of our societies. I have my preferences and objections, since my own mind, like everyone's, is dominated by many elements of what constitutes, for it, the normative order; but I know of no absolute and eternal authority for that order. I assume that, in the present stage of

4

our evolution, a normative order proper to one people in the condition in which it finds itself may not be proper to another in another condition. I do not believe that the world of man, which is still evolving, has arrived at any ultimate end in terms of a normative order applicable to the organization of his societies. If there is such an order, representing the one and only propriety for our kind as the order of the hive represents the one and only propriety for the honeybee, then our evolution, unlike that of the honeybee, is still some distance from its attainment.

In sum, I am disposed to believe that, as any civilization is an artifice created by our kind, so any normative order is an artificial complex of rules — many quite arbitrary, as in the case of some that govern table-manners — to maintain the discipline without which there could be no civilization or any tolerable, let alone rewarding life. Some such complex is necessary, but one may do as well as another.

What impresses me in the present state of mankind is the discrepancy between any normative order at all that we men try to realize and the necessary limits of our actual achievement. In our individual lives and in our societies we strive to realize normative orders of one sort or another, and our attempts all end in failure. But the failure is like the death that occurs in the mythology of so many agricultural societies, a death forever followed by resurrection, a winter forever followed by another spring. Although men always fail, they always try again; and we must hope that these alternating seasons of striving and failure are leading to some ultimate end, however distant.

I find it plausible to speculate that our Darwinian evolution, which determines our cultural as well as our physical development, is proceeding toward the destination of some normative order as established as that of the honeybee, a species that took the path of evolution to its end ahead of our own. In this view, the evolution of our species involves the progressive emergence over the centuries of the normative order, embracing individual behavior and social organization alike, that is proper to it.* In the interim, however, there is disagreement among us on what is the proper conduct of our lives, on what is the proper way for us to behave to one another, on what is the proper organization of our societies. This disagreement takes the form of conflicting normative orders, whether they present themselves as complete ideologies, as ethical systems, as models of political organization, or as modes of personal conduct. It is characteristic of them all, however, that our repeated attempts to enact them repeatedly fail before the recalcitrance of existential reality.

I would like to believe that we are now reaching a stage in our evolution when we can increasingly distinguish elements common to the disparate normative orders that represent, respectively, different cultures. Let me risk one example in the field of ethics.

Thucydides relates how, during the Peloponnesian War, an Athenian expedition conquered Melos. The Athenians, brutalized by years of fighting, ended by putting all the adult male Melians to death, then selling the women and children into slavery. Before they did this, however, the Melian spokesmen pleaded that the people be spared in the name of the generally accepted view of what constitutes justice. Thereupon a classic debate took place. Said the Athenians: "You know and we know, as practical men, that the question of justice arises only between parties equal in strength, and that the strong do what they can, and the weak submit. . . . We believe that Heaven, and we know that men, by a

---

*   I have presented this view more fully in two books, Men and Nations (Princeton, 1962 and 1965) and The Society of Man (New York, 1965 and 1969; London, 1965). For the basic distinction between the natural society of the beehive and the artificial societies of mankind see my Out of Chaos (Boston, 1977), pp. 294-295 and 489.

6

natural law, always rule where they are stronger. We did not make that law, nor were we the first to act on it; we found it existing, and it will exist for ever, after we are gone; and we know that you and anyone else as strong as we are would do as we do."

Here was a confrontation between two normative conceptions: the justice on the basis of which the Melians felt entitled to be spared, and what the Athenians called "natural law." Men who represented intellectual and moral authority at the time, and those who have represented it since, have been unanimous in supporting the normative position of the Melians and condemning that of the Athenians. Indeed, it is striking how the Melian outrage provoked anti-Athenianism among sensitive Athenians in much the same way that the Vietnamese War provoked anti-Americanism among Americans. The Athenian, Thucydides, identified the crime at Melos with the moral downfall of Athens that preceded its political and military downfall.

The most profound condemnation of the Athenian case, however, was put forward by another Athenian, Euripides, in his play, The Trojan Women, produced in Athens a few months after the obliteration of Melos. The Trojan Women presents the fall of Troy, but those who attended its performance would have had in mind, as the author had in mind, the fall of Melos. It displays the barbarous behavior of its author's fellow Greeks in killing the Trojan men and carrying the women off into slavery. The paradoxical message of the play is that the real victory, which is the moral victory, belonged to the Trojans who were killed or enslaved, while the Greeks had suffered a self-inflicted defeat. ("How are ye blind, ye treaders down of Cities . . . yourselves so soon to die !") The Trojan Women is remarkable because it equates true victory with fidelity to a normative conception, rather than with the victory that, confined to the existential world, will quickly turn to ashes in the mouths of those who taste it. The fall of the House of Atreus proceeds from the ostensible victory of the Atreides and their associates over the Trojans, just as

7

the fall of Athens is about to proceed from its ostensible victory over the Melians.

More than four centuries before the Christian era, then, we see the strong emergence of a conception that attaches the normative value of propriety to compassion, to mercy, and to moderation in victory. This normative conception has become more widely prevalent and more firmly established since the fifth century B.C. Twenty-five centuries earlier, we may be sure, it had no standing, except conceivably among some individuals in the Middle East or China. Twenty-five centuries later such genocide as was practiced on the Melians is universally condemned, and when it is occasionally practiced still, as it was by the Nazis, creates a scandal the world over. In this we may well believe that we see one example of the emergence of a normative order that may one day be unquestioned for all mankind, determining its conduct and the organization of its societies.

All that is relevant to the three following essays, however, is that they equate heroism and tragedy with the struggle of distinguished individuals to realize their respective visions of a normative order in an existential world that represents anarchy. In Hamlet and in Le Morte d'Arthur, the struggle ends in death, but with the hint of resurrection to come. In The Odyssey it ends with a limited success that will not endure (see the prophecy of Teiresias in Book 11). It is in these terms that all three are the expressions of a philosophy that, if we will take account of it, enables us to observe for once what we had seen every day.

Notes

The quotation that precedes this "General Introduction" is from Gilbert Murray's Euripides and his Age, London, 1946, page 160.

The quotation from J.-J. Rousseau in the first sentence is my translation from the twenty-first paragraph of the First Part of his Discours sur l'origine de l'inégalité parmi les hommes.

The citation from Thucydides is from his History of the Peloponnesian War, edited in translation by Sir R.W. Livingstone, London-New York-Toronto, 1943, 1946, Book V.

HAMLET AND THE WORLD

I. INTRODUCTION

Nor does Shakespeare seem to call for
explanations beyond those which a whole
heart and a free mind abundantly supply.

—Mark van Doren*

This comment on Hamlet was originally prompted by
the casual remark of a young man who had been brought
up on Shakespeare and had just taken a college course
on him. He said he could see the greatness of Macbeth
all right, but that Hamlet seemed to him meaningless—so
much so that he wondered whether its reputation wasn't
fraudulent. My first reaction was one of frustration. I
felt like someone who, longing to show a color-blind
friend the color green, knows how useless it would be to
try. Later, however, having been thus prompted to
think about the meaning of Hamlet, I had one of those
sudden accesses of assurance that are nearly always
delusory. I felt sure that I could, after all, show him
what it was. By going over the play with him line-by-
line, I could make him see with perfect clarity why it
was greater even than Macbeth. At last it occurred to
me that, in default of an opportunity to do this viva
voce, I could do it as well on paper—if not line-by-line
then scene-by-scene. Is it not just such a combination of
frustration and self-delusion that makes one ever write
anything at all ?

---

*   Shakespeare, New York, 1939, page 2.

My initial reaction to a casual remark had a long background. I had been reading Hamlet and seeing performances of it ever since I was a boy in New York. I doubt that I was more than twelve when I read it for the first time, in preparation for a performance to which my parents were taking my sister and me. I still remember our living-room and the big easy-chair in which I sat by myself, making what sense I could of the lines. (Almost surely I had already read the story in Charles and Mary Lamb's Tales from Shakespeare, which was the standard introduction for children of my generation.) What I do remember clearly is the gold-stamped red-leather pocket-book, hardly bigger than a man's hand, of the forty-volume Temple edition that my parents had, for I was to read it often through the years to come, while I was still at home and growing up. Over the past thirty to forty years I have been reading it in the Oxford edition of W.J. Craig; and lately I have been reading it as well in the Cambridge edition of J. Dover Wilson.

I also remember performances: one in modern dress, one without the cuts that are normally made, one in the movies (with Laurence Olivier), and others. All performances are unsatisfactory, if only because there is more to Hamlet's character than even the most intelligent actor, it seems, can get into a single performance. Generally the actor and the director interpret him narrowly, emphasizing some elements only. They are often tempted to make him excessively lively, presumably to ease the actor's task of holding his audience, and I have seen performances in which his soliloquies were constantly interrupted by something approaching acrobatics. (I daresay the Hamlet of II,2 would have had some caustic comment on this.) There has also been a tendency to insist that the view of Hamlet as a thoughtful and introspective person is wrong, that he is really a frustrated Napoleon whose overriding ambition is to get the throne of Denmark for himself. Apparently it is necessary to reduce him to a stock figure that anyone can understand.

However this may be, as I matured, and as the written play became a part of my being, I felt a dissatisfaction with every performance I saw. The initial frustration with which I reacted to the young man's remark was not new to me.

What I had forgotten until I was well along in this enterprise was that I had already had the idea, many years ago, of writing a book on Hamlet. Taking from my shelves one of the volumes of Furness's Variorum edition, I found inside it a sheaf of notes I had made for such a book. They were minutely detailed, reminding me that what I had intended doing then was something much bigger than what I was doing now.

I must make clear the limits of the present undertaking. It offers a personal view of what Hamlet means. This is something different from Shakespearian scholarship, to which it offers no contribution at all. Let me exemplify the distinction by noting that every page of Hamlet represents intellectual conceptions or attitudes peculiar to the England in which Shakespeare lived. Competent scholars, analyzing these elements, have shown how the play is relevant to its time and place, an undertaking for which I would be unqualified. The basis of its greatness, however, is that it transcends time and place. Its timeless and universal meaning, rather than its topical meaning, is what has concerned me here; and what I offer is only that meaning as it presents itself to one man with his own limitations of sensitivity, experience, and understanding—Hamlet as it seems to me.

In the course of setting down this personal commentary I was sometimes conscious of the disapproval that Dr. J. Dover Wilson, in particular, would feel for what I was doing. Dr. Wilson "in particular" because, by outdistancing all competitors in the constancy and thoroughness of his lifetime scholarship, he had come as near as any scholar can to making a work of literature his private possession. In What Happens in Hamlet* and

---

*   Cambridge, 1962.

15

in the Introduction to his edition of Hamlet* he put forward an eloquent case against the possibility of understanding Hamlet's character without first fully understanding the plot of the play, of fully understanding the plot without first understanding key passages in the dialogue, and of understanding the key passages without first achieving a complete mastery of the textual problems that the play presents. Having himself spent thirty or forty years preparing himself to understand Hamlet's character, he all but said that responsible comment on it requires no less.

As if this were not sufficiently intimidating in itself, Dr. Wilson reinforced his territorial claim by his strictures on "the psychological approach" to Hamlet's character. It is at this point, however, that I locate the chink in his armor. Even as one reads him—and other critics in the tradition of the schoolmen—it becomes apparent to one outsider, at least, that the subjective sympathy on which "the psychological approach" depends may make a contribution that could not be made by a lifetime of research into such questions as Elizabethan attitudes toward ghosts. For example, Hamlet's flippantly disrespectful responses to the voice of his father's spirit rising from the cellerage (I,5) pose a greater problem for Dr. Wilson and many of his compeers than they would for anyone who knew in himself, when others were present, the impulse to suppress by an outward flippancy an inner disposition to weep. Again, Dr. Wilson feels a need to explain, by artful elaborations of plot and action, Hamlet's offensive behavior to Ophelia in III,1—a need he would not feel if he credited him with the power of intuitive apprehension that another reader might take for granted in one so sensitive to the presence of evil. In sum, because the character of Hamlet is not psychologically plausible to many critics, for subjective reasons, they are driven to invent ingenious elaborations of the circumstances that constitute the plot in order to explain his actions. Standing back from the

---

* Cambridge, 1964.

16

play as I do, however, and taking not an analytic but a synoptic view of the world with Hamlet in it, I have decided that, while profiting by the researches of the schoolmen, I will not be intimidated. In this one respect, at least, I am arrogant in my unpretentiousness.

One can appreciate the character of Hamlet, I think, only to the extent that one is Hamlet oneself. No doubt this is equally true of all the real characters in literature, of Macbeth or Othello, of Don Quixote or Sancho Panza, of Dmitri Karamazov or Prince Andrey Bolkonsky. Hamlet, however, represents the solitary individual who does not share the common mind by which his environment is governed. It therefore seems to me out of the question that anyone who, sharing the common mind, is happily adjusted to his environment, could understand him. Many who read the play think it must be great, as they have been told it is, because its lines are sonorous and high-flung, or because there is a mystery about his "madness" as about the Mona Lisa's smile, but they take Hamlet to be something different from what he is. This is why he is interpreted on the stage so much more variously than Macbeth or Othello, Lear or Falstaff.

Again, men of the greatest intelligence who are, however, men of action rather than introspective contemplatives, could have no sympathetic understanding of Hamlet—could not, that is, identify with him. (For example, I cannot believe that the play could have held as much meaning as <u>King Henry V</u> for Sir Winston Churchill; and this appears to be true as well of Sir Laurence Olivier, who was memorable in the roles of Henry V and Hotspur.) One must suffer from a certain maladjustment to feel the reality of Hamlet.

Finally, there is the quality of Hamlet's mind. He is the prime example in fictional literature of intellect. Other heroes of Shakespearian tragedy—Lear, Othello, Macbeth, Antony—are capable of great passion or great moral nobility. Hamlet suffers and feels self-contempt because he is not capable of great passion, or of moral nobility in the conventional terms imposed by his environment. It is the quality of his mind that accounts for this incapacity. He is essentially solitary because he thinks and, thinking, cannot truly believe what everyone else believes; and because he therefore cannot, in any ultimate test, act on the common beliefs.

There are other examples in literature and history. Plato's Socrates is the first that comes to mind: the same opposition between him and his environment exists as in the case of Hamlet. Sir Thomas More is another; and he finally allowed himself to be beheaded, although he was offered an alternative, as Socrates finally allowed himself to drink the hemlock, although he too had been offered an alternative. Ahab, in Melville's Moby Dick, represents the same thing in symbolic terms. More often, however, it appears to be innocence or a peculiar incorruptibility, rather than intellectual brilliance, that casts such heroes in the role of isolation from their environments. This is the case with Voltaire's Candide; it is the case with Hassan and Ishak in James Elroy Flecker's Hassan. It is essentially the case with Huckleberry Finn confronting the moral issue involved in helping a slave escape from his owner. Both Candide and Huck think they must be deficient because they cannot meet the claims of the environment; but they are more intelligent than they know. The quality of the mind and its incorruptibility (often in spite of itself) are alike involved in every case; but in the case of Hamlet what stands out is the quality of the mind, and it is against his will that he cannot act by the common conceptions of his environment in obedience to the injunction laid on him by his father's spirit. An important part of his incorruptibility is un-conscious and even unwilling.

The implicit conclusion of what I have said might be that one must be exceptionally intelligent to appreciate Hamlet; but I shall at least qualify this by adding that the need is not for a great brain. I cannot believe that Socrates, by the standard tests, would have proved the best brain in Athens—that he would, say, have beaten everyone else in chess or in the solution of mathematical problems. When the Delphic oracle reported that there was no man wiser, he showed the peculiar quality of his intelligence by interpreting it to mean that his unique wisdom consisted in nothing more than the knowledge of his own ignorance. Men who can solve complicated mathematical problems in their heads will still live by the conventional beliefs of their environments, without questioning them, even when those beliefs make no sense. The intelligence that Socrates and Hamlet represent, each in his own way, is simply the intelligence that cannot accept without question, that has to think for itself at all hazards. More important than the possession of a great brain, for the appreciation of Hamlet, is the retention from childhood of the questioning innocence represented by the little child in Anderson's tale of "The Emperor's New Clothes."

There are, however, degrees of appreciation, corresponding to the degree in which each of us is Hamlet. That the play has, for almost four centuries, been generally regarded as one of the greatest monuments of literature shows how many of us must have at least a touch of Hamlet in us, however we may have succeeded in suppressing its appearance in public.

I shall pursue this discussion further in the wider commentary that follows the scene-by-scene exposition. At this point let me refer back to the statement, above, of the assurance I felt at the beginning that by such an exposition I could show the greatness of Hamlet. When I had completed the exposition and read it over I saw immediately that I had not succeeded. Those to whom the play means little or nothing will not find in this running commentary the revelation that, in my moment of excitement, I had expected to make. Those to whom it already means much will disagree with it to the extent that the meaning they have found is different; and if they don't disagree they will, perhaps, think it banal. I can still hope, however, that for all my readers there may be at least an occasional insight that enlarges their understanding. Those who, like the young man, had found the play without meaning may still get an inkling of impenetrable depths; and those for whom it already had meaning, if they do not find that meaning enlarged, may at least find that it has been helpfully formulated.

As I set down my running commentary it became evident to me that, within the limits of such a restrictive form, I could not explore the larger meaning of the play. If I was going to relate the court of Denmark to the world, then I would have to give an account of the world that showed the relevance, and I could not do this in the context of comments on individual scenes. The same problem arose if I was to identify the dilemma of Hamlet with dilemmas repeatedly faced by individuals over the centuries, and today as well. Therefore I added a general discussion, in the form of a further chapter, which contains the burden of what I want to say. The large meaning of <u>Hamlet</u> is to be found there more than in the running commentary that has now become preliminary to it. But it is still just the meaning that the play has for one man.

II.   THE PLAY

1.   <u>'Tis bitter cold, and I am sick at heart.</u>

Darkness outdoors, and figures moving in it.

Suddenly, like the sound of a shot: "Who's there ?"

"Nay, answer <u>me</u>; stand, and unfold <u>yourself</u>."

"Long live the king !"

The two men recognize each other by their voices and the brief crisis, with its note of panic, is over.

Francisco, an honest old soldier, has been standing sentry on the platform of the castle at Elsinore, alone in the blind dark and the cold, with "not a mouse stirring." Bernardo was simply coming to relieve him, the hour being midnight. The old soldier tells him: "For this relief much thanks; 'tis bitter cold, and I am sick at heart."

Already one has the impression of confusion, something wrong in Denmark. The intruder in the dark has challenged the sentry, who should have challenged him first; and now the sentry confides that he is sick at heart. There is insecurity in the atmosphere without, as yet, a known reason for it.

Unlike Francisco, Bernardo is to be joined by others in his watch, Horatio and Marcellus. Their voices sound in the darkness, hushed greetings are exchanged, and the honest old soldier retires thankfully to bed.

Of the four actors introduced in the first twenty lines of <u>Hamlet</u>, only Horatio is to have a significant role. Now, in his first brief line, he characterizes himself. To Bernardo's question in the dark, "What ! is Horatio there ?" he replies: "A piece of him." This relaxed good humor contrasts with the tension of the other actors. All through the play (except for one moment at the end) Horatio's serenity will remain unaffected by the charged atmosphere of Elsinore. The bitter cold will not penetrate him, nor will he be sick at heart. Insensitive to his surroundings and imperturbable—more an antique Roman than a Dane, as he says of himself—he will be a source of strength to the oversensitive Prince Hamlet. At a critical instant, when Hamlet needs an ally whose judgment he can trust as he cannot his own, he will tell him: "Horatio, thou art e'en as just a man as e'er my conversation cop'd withal." To this he will quickly add:

> Nay, do not think I flatter;
> For what advancement may I hope from thee,
> That no revenue hast but thy good spirits
> To feed and clothe thee ? Why should the poor be flattered ?
> No; let the candied tongue lick absurd pomp,
> And crook the pregnant hinges of the knee
> Where thrift may follow fawning.

So he makes it clear that he is not speaking in terms of the world identified with his uncle's court. Having done so, he continues:

> Since my dear soul was mistress of her choice
> And could of men distinguish, her election
> Hath sealed thee for herself; for thou hast been
> As one, in suffering all, that suffers nothing,
> A man that fortune's buffets and rewards
> Hast ta'en with equal thanks; and blessed are those
> Whose blood and judgment are so well co-mingled
> That they are not a pipe for fortune's finger
> To sound what stop she please. Give me that man
> That is not passion's slave, and I will wear him
> In my heart's core, ay, in my heart of heart,
> As I do thee.

Horatio is one of the three men who, because their characters are the opposite of Hamlet's, each in its own way, will arouse his special admiration. The other two are Fortinbras, the man who is able to act because he does not ruminate, and Laertes, who has no intellect to interfere with the crude impulses of passion. Hamlet will try especially, but in vain, to identify himself with the latter two. In a world that is entirely opposite to him, we shall, in fact, see him trying time and again to establish a bond with his opposites—with Horatio, with Rosencrantz and Guildenstern, with his mother, even with Laertes when he fights him, first in Ophelia's grave and again in the final scene. He will come nearest to succeeding with Horatio, the only one of them all who will not betray him, and who alone will remain in the end to speak for him before the new generation. But it is loyalty more than understanding that Horatio can give, since Hamlet's is not the common mind of our common understanding.

Meanwhile, the contrast between the tension of the environment and Horatio's relaxation has been introduced. Four words and we half know him already.

Now, with Francisco gone, Marcellus asks Bernardo: "What ! has this thing appeared again tonight ?" "This thing" must be connected with the fear and uncertainty, and with the fact that Bernardo is being reinforced in his watch.

2.   <u>Let us impart what we have seen tonight unto young Hamlet</u>.

Another twenty lines and the immediate cause of apprehension ("this thing") appears, in the form of an intrusion from another world. The basis of Hamlet's dilemma is, in fact, the opposition between two worlds, which in his mind are respectively represented by the King his father, now dead, and the King his uncle, now enthroned. Although the world of the former has been replaced by the world of the latter, it remains present in Hamlet's mind. He cannot bury it; he cannot quiet its appeal.

The intrusion from the other world is the ghostly semblance of Hamlet's father, which now reappears for a third successive night, passing in silence before the startled eyes of the watchers on the platform.

What does it signify ?

Horatio, Bernardo, and Marcellus are ordinary men. Like all ordinary men, they tend to accept as legitimate whatever world they find themselves in. They had, under the old King, accepted the world he represented, and they now accept as automatically the world of his successor. The return of the former King's semblance therefore represents a sort of usurpation, and their initial reaction is hostile. Horatio's first words to it are:

> What art thou that usurp'st this time of night,
> Together with that fair and warlike form
> In which the majesty of buried Denmark
> Did sometimes march ?

—whereupon he peremptorily commands it to speak, behaving toward it as if he were a game-keeper apprehending a poacher.

Although this represents the initial reaction of the watchers on the platform, it is not a confident reaction. Their feelings are bound to be contradictory, for they had respected the old King, and this semblance has all the majesty they had respected in him. On second thought, therefore, it does not seem right to treat it so cavalierly. "We do it wrong, being so majestical, to offer it the show of violence," says Marcellus after its departure.

The three are ordinary men, without special powers

of insight. The best they can do, by way of explaining this intrusion, is to speculate that the ghost has come to warn of some impending danger to the state. But Hamlet, who is not an ordinary man, will know immediately that the matter is not so simple. The information of his father's return will confirm suspicions that had been tormenting him all along.

Are the others quite without the same suspicions ?

Since Bernardo and Marcellus, who saw the apparition first, are officers of the castle guard, why did they not report its appearance, directly or through channels, to the new King ? Instead, they reported it to Horatio, who so far from having any position at court is simply a poor scholar recently arrived on a visit from Wittenberg. And now Horatio decides that it should be reported, immediately, not to the King but to Hamlet.

3.　　But now, my cousin Hamlet, and my son,—

The new King and his court, meanwhile, know nothing of what has begun to germinate in the dark like a seed. He has reached the pinnacle of success, and his self-confidence is at the full. Sitting upon what had so recently been his brother's throne, accompanied by the Queen who had so recently been his brother's Queen, attended by what had so recently been his brother's Lord Chamberlain, and surrounded by the court that had so recently waited upon his brother, he plays his new role, now, with a verbal virtuosity that approaches genius. His speech is beautiful like the movement of a snake, surely the greatest masterpiece of its kind in the English language:

> Though yet of Hamlet our dear brother's death
> The memory be green, and that it us befitted
> To bear our hearts in grief and our whole kingdom
> To be contracted in one brow of woe,
> Yet so far hath discretion fought with nature

That we with wisest sorrow think on him,
Together with remembrance of ourselves.
Therefore our sometime sister, now our queen,
The imperial jointress of this warlike state,
Have we, as 'twere with a defeated joy,
With one auspicious and one dropping eye,
With mirth in funeral and with dirge in marriage,
In equal scale weighing delight and dole,
Taken to wife: nor have we herein barred
Your better wisdoms, which have freely gone
With this affair along: for all, our thanks.

Then, rapidly disposing of some diplomatic business, he turns the power of his seductive art upon Laertes, son of his newly inherited Lord Chamberlain, Polonius, whose loyalty is still too fresh to be neglected:

What wouldst thou beg, Laertes,
That shall not be my offer, not thy asking ?
The head is not more native to the heart,
The hand more instrumental to the mouth,
Than is the throne of Denmark to thy father.
What wouldst thou have, Laertes ?

Laertes wants to return to France, and is given permission to do so. In the disposition of this second piece of business, his loyalty, together with his father's, is sealed.

This, however, was merely prelude to the chief business, to the solution of what is the new King's one remaining domestic problem. The entire court has accepted him in succession to his brother, has given itself to him completely, with one exception. While young Hamlet has dutifully gone through the same motions of loyalty as all the others, he still stands apart from the world that orbits, now, about the new King. Although the period of mourning has been terminated, he wears it still. Clad in black, he stands out from the rest, in implicit opposition to everyone else in the throne-room, a living reproach to the Queen his mother and to all the other members of the company who flatter the King with bright colors and an affected gaiety; and this but two months after the death of the old King, whom they had flattered with like semblances of devotion. He will give what lip-service he must, but he will not join their world. The new King's powers will not work on him as they have on Laertes and the rest.

"But now, my cousin Hamlet, and my son,—." The King starts hesitantly, and stops. Then: "How is it that the clouds still hang on you ?"

"Not so, my lord; I am too much in the sun." The King is left to weigh the implications of impertinence in this reply.

The Queen tries what she can do by pleading:

Do not for ever with thy vailed lids
Seek for thy noble father in the dust:
Thou knowest 'tis common; all that live must die,
Passing through nature to eternity.

Hamlet's response has its own power, contrasting with that of the King's sinuous verbal performances. "Ay, madam, it is common." The phrase strikes the ear like a single note, ended as soon as begun, but with overtones that survive it. Hamlet, one sees, is the rock on which the King's craft will at last founder.

The King returns to the charge, half flattering half scolding, and not neglecting the appeal to self-interest:

...for let the world take note,
You are the most immediate to our throne;
And with no less nobility of love
Than that which dearest father bears his son
Do I impart toward you.

Because the King can hope to win Hamlet over if he remains at the court, but not if he goes dissatisfied abroad, where he might become a center of disaffection, he opposes his desire to return to his university studies at Wittenberg. Since the King's wish has the effect of a command, although he is careful not to couch it in such terms, and since the Queen adds her entreaties, Hamlet acquiesces. His obedience, however, which he owes to the new King, is made only to his mother: "I shall in all my best obey you, madam."

If there is a slight to the King's authority he chooses to overlook it, accepting Hamlet's submission as if it had been ungrudging. He is overconfident, still, and now allows the streak of vulgarity to show in him. Nothing could be in worse taste than to proclaim, as he now does, a night of drinking and revelry in celebration of Hamlet's supposed surrender. "Why, 'tis a loving and a fair reply," he says. Then:

> Madam, come;
> This gentle and unforced accord of Hamlet
> Sits smiling to my heart; in grace whereof,
> No jocund health that Denmark drinks to-day,
> But the great cannon to the clouds shall tell,
> And the king's rouse the heavens shall bruit again,
> Re-speaking earthly thunder. Come away.

4.   But break, my heart, for I must hold my tongue !

Since it would be fatal to let others see all that he has inside him, Hamlet has to disguise his feelings, sometimes by putting on an antic disposition that will make people think him mad. As soon as he finds himself alone, however, he relieves himself in a flood of words. It is in his soliloquies, of which the first occurs now, upon the departure of the King and his court, that his inner conflict is revealed.

Of the two worlds that stand opposed in his mind, one is an ideal conceptual world, a normative world, a world of harmony, dignity, and truth, a world of propriety in which men and women are governed in their behavior to one another by a system of legitimate relationships that presents itself to the mind as God's or nature's plan. The other is an unbridled world; a world without harmony in which mutually contending men, obedient to no rules, are driven by their ambition for place and power; it is a world of licentiousness in which the animal appetites are freely indulged; it is a world of universal hypocrisy and deceit; it is the world of existential chaos that contrasts with the world of ideal order. This world it is that actually exists around him, while the other is an inner world of the creative and aspiring mind.

We should not ask, then, whether what moves Hamlet to such disgust and desperation is his mother's hasty marriage, or his uncle's usurpation of a throne that he had expected to occupy himself, or the failure to pay his father's memory the respect of an extended period of mourning, or some other topical occasion. The revulsion he feels is against the whole existential world to which these occasions belong. He is, however, indissolubly bound to that world by kinship and what we may call hieratic position. As he says himself, in the first phrase we hear from his lips, he belongs to it as kin but not as kind. Another man not occupying his position might seek to escape by entering a monastery. If he had been the son of Polonius he would have been free to return to Wittenberg, as Laertes was allowed to return to France. But he is the son of the deceased King of Denmark, the King who represented the legitimate world; and he is also the prince who, after the usurping King, stands first in the land. The only escape from his inherited obligations as the representative of legitimacy would be in death, which ends all wordly obligations, and so his thoughts turn naturally to death:

> O ! that this too too solid flesh would melt,
> Thaw and resolve itself into a dew;
> Or that the Everlasting had not fixed
> His canon 'gainst self-slaughter !

In this his first soliloquy his initial complaint is of the existential world in general:

How weary, stale, flat, and unprofitable
Seem to me all the uses of this world.
Fie on't ! O fie ! 'tis an unweeded garden,
That grows to seed; things rank and gross in nature
Possess it merely.

Only then does he particularize by citing, as examples, the impropriety of his mother's behavior, his uncle's vulgarity, and the offense to his father's memory.

It is clear that his own exclusion from the immediate succession is among his particular grievances; but everything in his character and attitude also shows that this is not a matter of personal ambition, of concern for his own personal advancement. The maintenance of the normative world's integrity had been the responsibility of the King his father, who had discharged it up to the moment of his death. He, as his father's natural heir and successor, might have expected to assume that responsibility in his turn, to bear in his turn the obligation of maintaining the normative order. Instead, however, his crafty and corrupt uncle has "popp'd in between the election and my hopes," the integrity of the order has been undone, the existential chaos has taken its place. "The time is out of joint," he will say; "O cursed spite, that ever I was born to set it right !" Meanwhile, however, "break, my heart, for I must hold my tongue !"

5.   . . . foul deeds will rise, though all the earth
                    o'erwhelm them, to men's eyes,

It is alone, still, after the departure of the King and court, that Horatio, Marcellus, and Bernardo find him. He is wrapped in his own thoughts, so much so that he has a moment of hesitation in recognizing his fellow student from Wittenberg. "I am glad to see you well," he says with automatic courtesy; and only then: "Horatio, or I do forget myself." All through the following conversation there is a slight incoherence in his language, as of a man whose mind is between two worlds. We shall see the growth of this tendency to abstract himself from his surroundings, to live in the harmonious and intelligent world of his own mind, until he finds the detachment from the existential world and the inner peace that mark him in the final scenes, as he advances to meet the doom toward which the whole drama of his life has been moving. In the end, in the midst of spreading disaster, he will have achieved a serenity quite beyond that of Horatio.

When Horatio tells him of the ghost, now, the news does not come to him altogether as a surprise, for it is in part a confirmation ("foul deeds will rise, though all the earth o'erwhelm them, to men's eyes"). As was to be expected, he determines to stand watch that night with the three others, to solicit the message that the ghost presumably reserves for him alone.

6.   Farewell, Ophelia. . . .

Intensity and suspense have been building up toward a dénouement now imminent. At this point, however, comes an interlude that is both charming and poignant. We are in the house of Polonius, where Laertes, about to leave for France, is saying goodbye to his sister Ophelia. Hamlet, it transpires, has been courting her, and now Laertes with his worldly experience warns her of the dangers against which she must be on her guard.

> Perhaps he loves you now,
> And now no soil nor cautel doth besmirch
> The virtue of his will; but you must fear,
> His greatness weighed, his will is not his own,
> For he himself is subject to his birth;
> He may not, as unvalued persons do,
> Carve for himself, for on his choice depends
> The safety and the health of the whole state.

31

This is good standard advice, which she receives grace-
fully, adding only (and there is a twinkle in this):

> But, good my brother,
> Do not, as some ungracious pastors do,
> Show me the steep and thorny way to heaven,
> Whiles, like a puffed and reckless libertine,
> Himself the primrose path of dalliance treads,
> And recks not his own rede.

At this point Polonius bustles in and is surprised to
find Laertes not yet gone. Polonius, because he shows
signs of dotage, is a figure of fun: he fancies in himself
a cleverness with words that, in his old age, is declining
into strained figures and mere garrulity. Insistent as he
now is that Laertes leave immediately ("Aboard, aboard,
for shame ! The wind sits in the shoulder of your sail,
and you are stayed for."), he cannot resist the self-
indulgence of holding him back to listen to a long string
of precepts.

Once Laertes is gone, Polonius in turn takes up
with Ophelia the question of Hamlet's attentions, but not
so kindly. In harsh terms he forbids her to have anything more to do with him, perhaps because he has in
mind the dangerous opposition in which Hamlet now
stands to his ruthless new master. He wounds her by
identifying Hamlet's honorable professions of love as
"springs to catch woodcocks." Ophelia is stricken, but
the possibility of doubting her father's judgment or of
disobeying him will never occur to her, even though
obedience will, in the end, break her heart.

The interlude is over.

7.   <u>O my prophetic soul</u> !

Obscurity, and figures moving in it. We are back
where we began, at midnight in the chill air on the platform of Elsinore castle. Now, twenty-four hours later,

the three figures moving in the darkness are Hamlet, Horatio, and Marcellus. From the castle come sounds of revelry punctuated by fanfares and the thunder of cannon. To Horatio's innocent question—"What does it mean, my lord ?"—Hamlet answers with disgust:

> The king doth wake to-night and takes his rouse,
> Keeps wassail, and the swaggering up-spring reels;
> And, as he drains his draughts of Rhenish down,
> The kettle-drum and trumpet thus bray out
> The triumph of his pledge.

Just then, by contrast with the image of the new King that Hamlet is evoking, the silent, sober, and dignified apparition of the old King glows in the darkness.

"Angels and ministers of grace defend us !" Hamlet has a characteristic moment of hesitation. Then, with an effort of will, in spite of his companions' fears and his own, he determines to follow where the apparition beckons him.

We may take the ghost for what it ostensibly is, or we may take it as a device of the stage to represent the apprehensions of those to whom it appears—that is, we may take it as having a being of its own outside the mind or we may take it as a mental image only. Other ghosts in Shakespeare (Banquo's, Caesar's) are no more than manifestations of uneasy conscience. Not only Hamlet, but Bernardo, Marcellus, and Horatio as well, may have experienced apprehensions of something wrong in what has happened, in the death of the King and his brother's succession, before ever they knew of the ghost. All the ghost does for Hamlet, at least, is to confirm antecedent suspicions, which will remain no more than suspicions, still, to the extent that it is possible to doubt its validity. Having a philosophical mind, Hamlet is a constant prey to epistemological doubts. He is bound to ask himself at every turning, like Socrates, how he can know what he knows. He is never sure he can trust his mind's eye.

Meanwhile, it is evident that he cannot enter into an easy relationship with this semblance of a father whom he has idealized in his memory. For the existential world, restored in whatever form and however briefly, can never quite match the idealized memory that succeeds it, which is why it is well that dead heroes never return. The abstracted memory of the old King represents one of the two polar extremes that dominate the drama; but his corporeal memory is less impressive. There is an equivocation here that will trouble Hamlet's speech and action almost to the end. It will find its expression no less in over-emphatic avowals of filial loyalty and determination to avenge his father's death than in the confession of his doubts.

The ghost, after committing Hamlet in advance to avenge it, recounts the circumstances of the murder that Hamlet, at least in his subconscious mind, had apprehended from the beginning:

> Now, Hamlet, hear:
> 'Tis given out that, sleeping in mine orchard,
> A serpent stung me; so the whole ear of Denmark
> Is by a forged process of my death
> Rankly abused; but know, thou noble youth,
> The serpent that did sting thy father's life
> Now wears his crown.

"O my prophetic soul !" is Hamlet's instant response.

Now that he has at last had to recognize the fact of the crime, now that it has risen so explicitly into his conscious mind, Hamlet is committed to avenge it as he was not before. From now on, however, the conflict within him between the claims of the normative world and those of the existential will become complicated and take on an equivocal character. For the normative world of every man is in some degree different from that of every other, and is always in some degree beset by its own uncertainties and contradictions. In the normative world upheld by the orthodoxy of Hamlet's day, and represented by his father's spirit, every slight or injury is to be avenged by the sword. The ideal man, the hero, is the chivalric warrior who, in pursuance of a conventional conception of honor, plies his sword without such exercise of reflective thought as would inhibit its action. From now on, the conflict within Hamlet will involve, to his mind, the issue of courage or cowardice—an issue that will be made uncertain, however, by a persistent grain of philosophical doubt. For Hamlet is too intelligent and too modern to accept implicitly the conventional conceptions for which his father stood, however much he reveres his memory. (It is not uncommon for men who have, as a matter of moral allegiance, dedicated them-selves to causes for which their fathers stood, to suffer from increasing difficulty, as their minds mature, in maintaining their intellectual allegiance. John Stuart Mill is one example.)

8.   Hamlet, remember me.

A man who in his childhood had learned to identify moral authority with his father is likely, in later life, to have a conscience that is associated with his father's memory. He will be moved to live up to what his father would have expected of him, and to the extent that he fails he will feel himself guilty of filial betrayal.

The ghost's last words, as it fades out, are: "Hamlet, remember me." It is the voice of conscience touching the sense of guilt; and Hamlet, conscience-stricken, overdoes his response so that it does not ring true even to himself:

O all you host of heaven ! O earth ! What else ?
And shall I couple hell ? O fie ! Hold, hold, my heart !
And you, my sinews, grow not instant old,
But bear me stiffly up ! Remember thee !
Ay, thou poor ghost, while memory holds a seat
In this distracted globe. Remember thee !
Yea, from the table of my memory
I'll wipe away all trivial fond records,

All saws of books, all forms, all pressures past,
That youth and observation copied there;
And thy commandment all alone shall live
Within the book and volume of my brain,
Unmixed with baser matter: yes, by heaven
O most pernicious woman !
O villain, villain, smiling, damned villain !
My tables, —meet it is I set it down,
That one may smile, and smile, and be a villain;
At least I'm sure it may be so in Denmark.

On another occasion, when he has been assuaging his conscience with words in like manner, he will suddenly stop at the pinnacle of his stridency and say:

Why, what an ass am I ! This is most brave
That I, the son of a dear father murdered,
Prompted to my revenge by heaven and hell,
Must, like a whore, unpack my heart with words,
And fall a-cursing, like a very drab,
A scullion !

9.   These are but wild and whirling words, my lord.

From the moment that he has heard the ghost's secret Hamlet must dissemble, if only because it would be fatal if the King found out that he knew it. Unlike most of the court, however, he is untalented in hypocrisy. He had not disguised his continuing grief and consternation at his father's death, although it would have been politic to do so, and it is not likely now that he could put on an apparent serenity in the presence of the King. What will be safer is for him to feign a madness in which he seems, at worst, harmless and not responsible for his words. Where he cannot trust himself to maintain the appearance of impassivity, it will be better for him to rant and be rude.

He assumes such behavior now, as Horatio and Marcellus find him, bemusing them with "wild and whirling words," referring to the ghost in language that is light-hearted and impertinent. Both of them, however, are already in on the secret to the extent of knowing that he has received a communication from what is ostensibly his father's spirit, and neither will prove unworthy of trust. Therefore Hamlet changes his tune. Swearing them not to reveal what they have seen, he also requires them, if he should think meet thereafter "to put an antic disposition on," not to indicate that they know the cause of it.

Horatio, in any case, is the one person who will have his full confidence.

10. That hath made him mad.

Again tension is relaxed by an interlude in Polonius's house. The old fox instructs his confidential servant, Reynaldo, to spy on his son in Paris: he should get those acquainted with Laertes to reveal the truth about his conduct by attributing to him imagined faults of behavior that they will either confirm or deny.

Your bait of falsehood takes this carp of truth;
And thus do we of wisdom and of reach,
With windlasses, and with assays of bias,
By indirections find directions out.

In Polonius's language the word "wisdom" means the wisdom of serpents. This is the King's wisdom as well, and the wisdom of the court, which in one instance at least will prevail over the innocence of the dove.

Exit, then, Reynaldo, and enter Ophelia. She is in a state bordering on hysteria, reporting that Hamlet has come to her in disarray, his behavior that of a madman.

Polonius asks whether she has given him any hard words of late; to which she replies that, in obedience to his command, "I did repel his letters and denied his access to me."

"That hath made him mad," says Polonius, laying one finger to the side of his nose. . . . "Come, go we to the king: this must be known."

The King, at this same time, is busy with the devices of his own wisdom. Having sent to Wittenberg for Rosencrantz and Guildenstern, two of Hamlet's school-mates, he instructs them to spy on him. They should find out the cause of his altered behavior by drawing him on to pleasures, ingratiating themselves with him, and at last gaining his confidence.

Exeunt, then, the two spies, and enter Polonius to report "that I have found the very cause of Hamlet's lunacy." Polonius is now in his element, holding the King and Queen in impatient suspense while he indulges in a display of his penchant for devising empty figures of speech and convolutions of wit:

> My liege, and madam, to expostulate
> What majesty should be, what duty is,
> Why day is day, night night, and time is time,
> Were nothing but to waste night, day, and time.
> Therefore, since brevity is the soul of wit,
> And tediousness the limbs and outward flourishes,
> I will be brief.

At last, after more flights and flourishes, he reveals what he takes to be the truth: Hamlet, in the ecstasy of love, repulsed by Ophelia on her father's instruction that "Lord Hamlet is a prince, out of thy star," has declined "into the madness wherein now he raves."

To prove the point, Polonius proposes a test:

> I'll loose my daughter to him;
> Be you and I behind an arras then;
> Mark the encounter; if he love her not,
> And be not from his reason fallen thereon,

Let me be no assistant for a state,
But keep a farm, and carters.

"We will try it," says the King.

So here are the King and his Lord Chamberlain
about to assume the role of spies, while the poor pigeon
that is the latter's daughter is to be put to bait.

The King and Queen go off; Hamlet comes on, and
Polonius, after some exchanges of nonsense with Hamlet,
goes off to contrive the encounter Hamlet is to have with
the obedient Ophelia, whom he will at the proper moment
loose to him.

11.   <u>Gentlemen, you are welcome to Elsinore</u>.

Now comes a scene that should be sheer delight,
were we not aware of the undercurrent. Rosencrantz and
Guildenstern encounter Hamlet, who is spontaneously
overjoyed to see them. Wittenberg is where he longs to
be, and any fellow students arriving from that city
therefore find a special welcome. There is an echo, now,
of the spontaneous warmth with which he had earlier
welcomed Horatio. As in the case of Horatio, prince
though he is he will not receive these schoolmates as
servants but as friends.

Rosencrantz and Guildenstern, however, are a
different breed from Horatio: light-hearted and light-
headed, "as the indifferent children of the earth," full
of games and gaiety. Within an instant of the meeting, a
banter at once delicate and bawdy is engaged between
the two and Hamlet, showing a side of his nature we had
not seen before. Reminded by their presence of
Wittenberg, to which he may not return, he goes on to
refer to Denmark as a prison. This only provides these
eternal schoolboys with occasion for more banter.

"But, in the beaten way of friendship," Hamlet asks

(and the undercurrent begins to be felt), "what make you at Elsinore ?"

ROSENCRANTZ. To visit you, my lord; no other occasion.

HAMLET. Beggar that I am, I am even poor in thanks; but I thank you: and sure, dear friends, my thanks are too dear a half-penny. Were you not sent for ? Is it your own inclining ? Is it a free visitation ? Come, come, deal justly with me: come, come; nay, speak.

GUILDENSTERN. What should we say, my lord ?

HAMLET. Why anything, but to the purpose. You were sent for; and there is a kind of confession in your looks which your modesties have not craft enough to colour: I know the good king and queen have sent for you.

ROSENCRANTZ. To what end, my lord ?

HAMLET. That you must teach me. But let me conjure you, by the rights of our fellow-ship, by the consonancy of our youth, by the obligation of our ever-preserved love, and by what more dear a better proposer could charge you withal, be even and direct with me, whether you were sent for or no !

ROSENCRANTZ. [Aside to Guildenstern.] What say you ?

HAMLET. [Aside.] (Nay, then, I have an eye of you.) If you love me, hold not off.

GUILDENSTERN. My lord, we were sent for.

HAMLET. I will tell you why; so shall my

40

anticipation prevent your discovery, and your secrecy to the king and queen moult no feather. I have of late,—but wherefore I know not,—lost all my mirth, forgone all custom of exercises; and indeed it goes so heavily with my disposition that this goodly frame, the earth, seems to me a sterile promontory; this most excellent canopy, the air, look you, this brave o'erhanging firmament, this majestical roof fretted with golden fire, why, it appears no other thing to me but a foul and pestilent congregation of vapours. What a piece of work is a man ! How noble in reason ! how infinite in faculty ! in form, in moving, how express and admirable ! in action how like an angel ! in apprehension how like a god ! the beauty of the world ! the paragon of animals ! And yet, to me, what is this quintessence of dust ? man delights not me; [and then, in response to the trembling of a smile on Rosencrantz's lips] no, nor woman neither, though, by your smiling, you seem to say so.

In this scene we see Hamlet himself becoming in-creasingly crafty; and from now on, until he at last encompasses their destruction, he will not find it hard to outwit these two popinjays. The King, moreover, will not know that he knows them to be his agents.

12. The actors are come hither, my lord.

Rosencrantz and Guildenstern report that on their way to Elsinore they encountered a group of traveling actors, who are now coming to offer Hamlet service. They are the same tragedians of the city of Wittenberg that he had formerly delighted in; but they have had to take to the road because a change of fashion has favored another and less dignified school of players. "It is not very strange," says Hamlet; "for my uncle is King of Denmark, and those that would make mows at him while my father lived, give twenty, forty, fifty, a hundred ducats a-piece for his picture in little."

Again, however, he is overjoyed at the arrival of visitors who come, in his eyes, trailing clouds of glory, reminders of the days of his innocence in Wittenberg. For the moment the spirit of student gaiety prevails. Polonius, entering to announce the arrival of the players in his usual grandiloquent fashion, is unmercifully mocked by a Hamlet who has reverted to irresponsible boyhood, and who can now say under cover of his reputed madness what he might otherwise have to restrain.

The players arrive and, as in the case of the previous arrivals from Wittenberg, they are welcomed not as servants but as "friends." Hamlet eagerly begs the First Player to recite a speech he remembers having heard from him that describes the murder of King Priam in the presence of his horrified queen, Hecuba. The old actor does so with such feeling that, before the end, his color has changed and his eyes are brimming. Even Polonius is so shaken that he asks to have the performance stopped.

The speech has, suddenly, changed the mood of the scene. Speaking once more in sober and subdued tones, Hamlet asks Polonius to show the players to their quarters—and to use them well.

"My lord," says Polonius, "I will use them according to their desert."

No, Hamlet replies, use them much better. "Use every man after his desert, and who should escape whipping ? Use them after your own honour and dignity: the less they deserve, the more merit is in your bounty." His reply is worth citing because what is notable about Hamlet is the quality of his mind, which is distinguished by an ethical sophistication that, in lifting him above his surroundings, makes him the essentially solitary figure that he is.

To the players Hamlet now says: "Follow that lord" —and then, seeing in their eyes the mockery that, in his momentary frolic, he had given them a precedent for, he adds in a tone of compassion that is new: "and look you mock him not."

13. The play's the thing. . .

Alone again, Hamlet relieves his newly aroused anguish by again indulging himself in a flood of words that, as in the earlier soliloquy, will at last rise in violence until it is out of all measure.

> O ! what a rogue and peasant slave am I:
> Is it not monstrous that this player here,
> But in a fiction, in a dream of passion,
> Could force his soul so to his own conceit
> That from her working all his visage wann'd,
> Tears in his eyes, distraction in's aspect,
> A broken voice, and his whole function suiting
> With forms to his conceit ? and all for nothing !
> For Hecuba !
> What's Hecuba to him or he to Hecuba
> That he should weep for her ? What would he do
> Had he the motive and the cue for passion
> That I have ? He would drown the stage with tears,
> And cleave the general ear with horrid speech,
> Make mad the guilty and appal the free,
> Confound the ignorant, and amaze indeed
> The very faculties of eyes and ears.

He accuses himself of cowardice:

> . . . it cannot be
> But I am pigeon-livered, and lack gall
> To make oppression bitter, or ere this
> I should have fatted all the region kites

With this slave's offal.

And so he is off, at last, in a stream of shouted
vituperation against the "smiling, damned villain" of his
earlier ranting, calling him: "Bloody, bawdy villain !
Remorseless, treacherous, lecherous, kindless villain !"
This time, however, he stops short, suddenly conscious
that his ranting is childish, ashamed that instead of
acting he should, "like a whore, unpack my heart with
words. . . ."

Now he reverts to a plan that had entered his mind
as he listened to the First Player's speech. It is a plan
for at least preliminary action, but at the same time it is
a plan to defer action. His philosophic doubt is the
excuse for not proceeding immediately to fulfill the
promise that he will avenge his father's death:

> The spirit that I have seen
> May be the devil: and the devil hath power
> To assume a pleasing shape; yea, and perhaps
> Out of my weakness and my melancholy—
> As he is very potent with such spirits—
> Abuses me to damn me. I'll have grounds
> More relative than this: . . . .

His mind may have misled him, his apprehensions
may be illusions. So he plans to have the players re-
enact before the King the murder of Hamlet's father,
thereby trapping the King, if he is guilty, into betraying his guilt.

> . . . the play's the thing
> Wherein I'll catch the conscience of the king.

14. <u>And thus the native hue of resolution is sicklied o'er
with the pale cast of thought . . .</u>

The King and Polonius, having set Ophelia out as
bait for Hamlet, have hidden themselves to observe the

consequences. In the moment before Ophelia obediently comes on, Hamlet is seen alone with his own thoughts (which the hidden observers cannot read). "To be, or not to be," he muses: "that is the question:

> Whether 'tis nobler in the mind to suffer
> The slings and arrows of outrageous fortune,
> Or to take arms against a sea of troubles,
> And by opposing end them ?

This is a far cry from his earlier vows to avenge his father. He is weighing, here, the nobility of resignation, which implies an acceptance of his defeat by the whole existential world that his uncle represents, against defiance and action to set matters right. In the natural process of his thought, although by no strict logic, the question becomes one of death or continued living. As must always be the case with one who finds himself inescapably part of a world with which he cannot establish any personal bond, a world with which he is fated to be at odds, but which is bound to impose itself on him rather than be reformed, and who therefore finds himself under a strain that is incessant and exhausting, he is in love with the thought of death, the only escape:

> To die: to sleep;
> No more; and, by a sleep to say we end
> The heart-ache and the thousand natural shocks
> That flesh is heir to, 'tis a consummation
> Devoutly to be wished.

A man who expects defeat will come to look forward to it: he will look forward to the realization of his fears that ends them.

How can he know, however, that the realization will, in fact, end them ?

> To die, to sleep;
> To sleep: perchance to dream: ay, there's the rub;
> For in that sleep of death what dreams may come
> When we have shuffled off this mortal coil,

Must give us pause.

He is in a peaceful, abstracted, ruminative mood now, by contrast with the frenzy of his two earlier soliloquies. The only reason for continuing to bear the burden of a life that one could so easily end is that

> the dread of something after death,
> The undiscovered country from whose bourn
> No traveller returns, puzzles the will,
> And makes us rather bear those ills we have
> Than fly to others that we know not of.

This brings him back to the filial obligation on which he is defaulting, to his guilt, to the issue of courage and cowardice. The contemplation of death, and the fear that it arouses in contemplation, is, he muses, the real cause of cowardice:

> Thus conscience does make cowards of us all;
> And thus the native hue of resolution
> Is sicklied o'er with the pale cast of thought,
> And enterprises of great pith and moment
> With this regard their currents turn awry,
> And lose the name of action.

This is the first explicit statement of what is Hamlet's central problem: the opposition between thought and action. Every final decision involves an irrevocable renunciation of alternatives. This does not trouble those who make their decisions in action, without pausing for thought. Those, however, whose disposition is to weigh alternatives in advance, exploring them successively in the mind, learn that, since one can never complete such explorations, this may be a process without end that, by indefinitely deferring decision, results in no decision. Especially where issues of life and death are involved, the contemplation of what one risks in the adoption of any particular course of action, and of the possibilities that one foregoes in rejecting its alternatives, tends to paralyze action. Inaction, then, becomes the choice that makes itself by default.

For Hamlet, avenging his father's death means killing his uncle. If his uncle were not the King, he could, one supposes, compell him to fight a duel. In default of this possibility, however, there is, in Hamlet's mind, only that of taking him by surprise and cutting him down before help can reach him. Against this kind of killing there is a strong animal instinct, which exists in all vertebrates and not least in man (as Dr. Konrad Lorenz has shown in the last chapter of his book, King Solomon's Ring).

Hamlet's father, primarily a fighting man, would presumably have killed the usurper at whatever risk, and this is what he would have expected his son to do as a simple matter of honor. The impulsive Laertes, whose emotions govern a mind that hardly functions at all, would also have done so without thought. So would Fortinbras, who in this disposition is, more properly than Hamlet, heir to the old King. But Hamlet is a rare and different kind of man, a man dominated by a mind that can never truly accept the simple concepts and the crude values that prevail in his environment. If he accepts, at the surface of his consciousness, the common view of what constitutes honor and what honor requires, he does not believe in it profoundly and he does not accept it blindly. We all tend to accept certain attitudes that pass for noble among the generality of men as long as the honoring of them in action does not involve terrible consequences. When it does, we may find that what we had accorded them was more lip-service than true belief. The guilt Hamlet feels is in his inability to live up to his father's expectation that he will behave like a simple man of chivalry who does not let the uses of the mind subvert the common identification of honor with the sword. It is not a coincidence that the author of Hamlet lived in the same age as Machiavelli and Cervantes, two men who each in different ways proclaimed that the old concepts of chivalry were outdated. Hamlet is modern man before his time.

Be it noted, then, that Hamlet is at odds with his father's world as well as with his uncle's. In the trouble of his mind there are depths below depths.

Finally, this soliloquy is remarkable in showing another aspect of Hamlet's modernity. Elsewhere he uses the common language to express the common belief in an after-life in which punishment and reward are meted out, in which the assignment of immortal souls is made to Heaven or to Hell. He superficially believes what everyone around him believes. But at the more profound levels of his mind, as we see in this soliloquy, he is a modern agnostic almost three centuries before the word was coined.

15. <u>Those that are married already,</u>
<u>all but one, shall live . . .</u>

In this soliloquy at the beginning of the third act Hamlet manifests for just a moment the detachment and serenity that will increasingly be his as he approaches his death in the final act. He withdraws, for the moment, from the existential world into the world of his own mind, finding refuge in the philosophical contemplation of death. At the end of the soliloquy, however, he is abruptly brought back to the existential world—not by the entrance of Ophelia in itself, but by something constrained in her manner that, intuitively understood, arouses in him a sudden horror and revulsion.

So far Ophelia had seemed untainted by her sordid environment. Now, however, she comes to him in the same role as Rosencrantz and Guildenstern, as a dissembling agent of the new King, of his court and his corruption. If Hamlet had had a mixed reaction when his two schoolmates had been loosed on him, what must his reaction be now, when he perceives that Ophelia, too, is in the service of his enemies, performing a part that has been prepared for her, lending herself to the purpose of entrapping him !

His reaction of horror and disgust is expressed in a spate of bitterness against the poor girl who, with no mind of her own, is simply acting in obedience to authority that is, for her, unquestionable. His diatribe about the incompatibility of beauty and honesty has implications that go beyond the occasion. One is aware of a resonance, in his mind, between Ophelia's present betrayal and his mother's betrayal. The pristine virtue of each has been corrupted by the seductive influence of the new King. Each in her own way has been brought into his service, to be used against him as against his father.

The resonance, however, is not limited to the two female characters in Hamlet's life, the mature and the innocent, the mother and the girl who should have been his bride. It involves the very sin of Adam in his own soul, his awareness of the universal corruption in himself as in others. For beneath the ideal love of woman is the impulse that identifies a man with the beasts. In this light, beauty seemingly associated with innocence may suddenly appear as the opposite of innocent. "Wise men," Hamlet tells her, "know well enough what monsters you make of them." The innocent beauty of the girl is merely the trap that women set for men; and he is the more aware of this because one of the horrors with which he has been living is his knowledge that an adulterous appetite in his mother had played its part in drawing her from the old King to the new. Because he knows this appetite in himself, because his thoughts of Ophelia have not been innocent, his disgust with a world that uses that appetite for political purposes includes self-disgust.

> Get thee to a nunnery [he tells Ophelia]:
> why wouldst thou be a breeder of sinners ?
> I am myself indifferent honest; but yet I
> could accuse me of such things that it were
> better my mother had not borne me. . . .
> What should such fellows as I do crawling
> between heaven and earth ?

Here the whole identification of sexual attraction with moral corruption, which has been dominant in two thousand years of the Christian tradition—from St. Paul to the aged Tolstoy—is expressed with a sort of fury made more passionate by Hamlet's awareness of the fact that the betrayal by his mother and the betrayal by Ophelia are betrayals of which he is not himself innocent. In a final spasm of revulsion he shouts at Ophelia:

> Go to, I'll no more on't; it hath made me
> mad. I say, we will have no more marriages;
> those that are married already, all but one,
> shall live; the rest shall keep as they are.
> To a nunnery, go.

16. Madness in great ones must not unwatched go.

Poor Ophelia can have no perception of what is troubling Hamlet. She cannot see beneath his wild words, which seem merely to confirm her father's diagnosis of madness. "O, what a noble mind is here o'erthrown !" she exclaims as soon as Hamlet has left her, and then expresses her distress in a string of mis-applied banalities. The Hamlet she used to know is described in terms of a schoolgirl's understanding: he is "the glass of fashion and the mould of form."

With the wisdom of the serpent, however, the eavesdropping King has understood well enough what underlies Hamlet's words. In particular, he has not missed Hamlet's Parthian shot about "those that are married already, all but one . . .". He immediately rejects the superficial diagnosis that Polonius had offered:

> Love ! his affections do not that way tend;
> Nor what he spake, though it lacked form a little,
> Was not like madness. There's something in his soul
> O'er which his melancholy sits on brood;
> And, I do doubt, the hatch and the disclose

Will be some danger; which for to prevent,
I have in quick determination
Thus set it down: he shall with speed to England,
For the demand of our neglected tribute:
Haply the seas and countries different
With variable objects shall expel
This something-settled matter in his heart,
Whereon his brains still beating puts him thus
From fashion of himself.

The King, as we shall learn, has in mind that Hamlet shall not survive his trip to England; but he confides in Polonius no further than is needful.

For his part, the senile fox is crestfallen to have his theory of Hamlet's madness rejected by the King, and hopes still to have it confirmed. The possibility of simultaneously curing Hamlet's madness and making a brilliant match for his daughter, without seeming to conspire to that end, cannot have been excluded from his thoughts. He proposes, now, another test, this time using Hamlet's mother as bait in place of Ophelia— himself, once more, in his favorite place behind the arras.

Let his queen mother all alone entreat him
To show his griefs: let her be round with him;
And I'll be placed, so please you, in the ear
Of all their conference. If she find him not,
To England send him, or confine him where
Your wisdom best shall think.

To which the King replies:

It shall be so:
Madness in great ones must not unwatched go.

The play has arrived, at last, at the point where all the plot is unfolded and the conflict joined. Hamlet has undertaken, with whatever doubts and evasions, to kill his usurping uncle. The uncle, now sure enough of Hamlet's intention, will set a trap whereby to kill him first. From this point on, the actors are carried along by the schemes they have already devised. First there must be the play, already scheduled, by which Hamlet hopes to catch the conscience of the King. Then there must be the meeting with his mother, projected by Polonius. Then Hamlet must be bundled off to England and the trap that will await him there. What has so far been all talk has moved forward, now, to the stage of action, from which there can no longer be any turning back.

17.   . . . to show virtue her own feature, scorn her own image, and the very age and body of the time his form and pressure.

In the duel between Hamlet and the King, the first thrust is to be Hamlet's. Now that the moment for action (of a sort) has come at last, his mood changes. The composition and direction of a play is a congenial pursuit in which he is at home, as he would not be directing, say, a battle or a political campaign. His gifts are those of a literary man, not of a man of action. His vocation is "to show virtue her own feature, scorn her own image, and the very age and body of the time his form and pressure." Again, for a moment, the tension of the drama is unwound as he instructs the players in how to play the parts he has written for them. In language that is at once conversational and eloquent, he shows the radiance of his mind.

This scene with the players is pure sunshine. After the blackness of the preceding scene with Ophelia, the charm of his kindness and courtesy is a magic upon us— as when he had first welcomed the players. As at his first meeting with Rosencrantz and Guildenstern, he shows himself moved by a love of people the grace of which expresses itself in his language. He is at ease with the players as he can never be with the King and his court. He is equally at ease with his fellow student Horatio, also an outsider to the court, whose confidential support and assistance he invokes, in terms already cited, after the players have retired to make themselves ready.

18. The players cannot keep counsel; they'll tell all.

King, Queen, and courtiers now assemble to see Hamlet's play, taking their proper places. Hamlet, although his proper place is with the King and Queen, refuses the Queen's invitation to occupy it and, instead, places himself in opposition to them at the foot of the improvised stage, where Ophelia is modestly sitting. This is his program, he is master of the event, and the antic disposition he now puts on has an anticipatory note of triumph in it. He relieves the inner tension that is again mounting in him by deliberately outrageous behavior, profiting by the scope his pretended madness gives him. At the outset he embarrasses Ophelia by offering to lie in her lap and, when she blushingly demurs, asking with feigned surprise whether she had taken his meaning in an improper sense. She is young, however, and the boyishness he puts on is infectious. Too simple to catch the implications of crisis beneath his playfulness, bewildered and afraid and yet half happy to see him so young and merry himself, she begins to respond in kind.

No one else, we may be sure, misses the undertones of his merriness. He is in a sort of ecstasy at the discomfort he is now causing the King and Queen, at having them in a sense at his mercy—so much so that he cannot sit back and let the play serve its purpose by speaking for itself.

Spontaneously brilliant as Hamlet is on every occasion, he is incapable of the dissimulation required for political maneuver. His impulsive mind constantly reveals itself as sparks fly from a fire. The King, the Queen, and Polonius are alerted, even before the play begins, by his remark to Ophelia, which they are deliberately allowed to overhear: "What should a man do but be merry ? for, look you, how cheerfully my mother looks, and my father died within's two hours." Deep as he is, now, in the toils of a life-and-death conspiracy, he cannot exercise the self-restraint on which success would depend. Hamlet, although not really mad, does have moments of ecstasy that approach a madness akin to genius.

The ostensible objective of the play is to test the ghost's account of the old King's murder by playing it out in front of the supposed murderer, who could hardly avoid betraying himself by his reaction if the account should be true. But, before it ever comes to the murder, the old play Hamlet has rewritten for this purpose has made its theme that of a queen's sinful second marriage to the king who has taken her dead husband's place. In this alone there would be cause for an alarmed reaction by the King, as by the Queen, even if he had not committed the murder that the play goes on to depict. One must suppose that in writing it Hamlet was moved by something more than his desire to test the ghost's report.

In fact, Hamlet's device of the play is an evasion on his part. It is a substitute for the vengeance that a conventional honor, as well as obedience to his father's memory, would require him to take. Instead of killing the usurping King, for which he lacks the resolution, he seeks to discharge his obligation and his hatred by tormenting him with guilty fear. He wants the King to know that he knows, and to be afraid. The King's fear of him, then, should in itself tend to salvage Hamlet's self-respect, putting him in the superior position. By the device of the play, Hamlet is telling the King that he has not been fooled.

In the first exchange between Hamlet and the King, then, Hamlet has warned and wounded the King without incapacitating him. A better conspirator would have bewared of that.

There is no doubt, however, that Hamlet's thrust has gone home. The King could not have known until now that he was moved by more than revulsion at his mother's hasty and improper marriage, or by disappointment at not himself achieving the throne. Now he learns that the murder itself is known to him in full. An hour earlier, the complete success of his conspiracy to acquire his brother's throne and Queen alike had seemed confirmed, troubled only by Hamlet's emotional inability to reconcile himself to it, and the King had been confident that he could deal with that. Now all is suddenly and imminently threatened. By the device of the play Hamlet has virtually made public, before the court, the means by which the King has usurped his brother's place. For the first time we see the King in panic. No longer master of himself, he cries for lights and rushes from the hall. Hamlet is in an ecstasy of triumph.

19. <u>And now I'll do't</u>.

What follows comes so fast that the actions pile up on one another.

The King in alarm can no longer wait to strike against Hamlet. He must get him off to England immediately, accompanied by Rosencrantz and Guildenstern, who will carry sealed orders for his death. The two newly fledged courtiers respond to his excited instructions with obsequious eagerness, flattering him and themselves that, in acting to save his life, they will be saving the Kingdom. "The cease of majesty dies not alone," Rosencrantz says to him:

> but, like a gulf doth draw
> What's near it with it; it is a massy wheel,
> Fixed on the summit of the highest mount,
> To whose huge spokes ten thousand lesser things
> Are mortised and adjoined, which, when it falls,
> Each small annexment, petty consequence,

Attends the boisterous ruin. Never alone
Did the King sigh, but with a general groan.

(The point would have been apt if it had been applied to
the legitimate and murdered King.) To Guildenstern it is
"most holy and religious fear . . . to keep those many
bodies safe that live and feed upon your majesty." The
corrupting influence of power, whether with or without
virtue, is here epitomized. Hitler had around him men
like Rosencrantz and Guildenstern.

As the two leave, Polonius hurries in, informs the
King that Hamlet is already on the way to his mother's
chamber where he, Polonius, will be hidden behind the
arras, and hurries out again. The King hardly heeds
what has now become irrelevant.

Left alone, he has a moment of fearful and des-
pairing introspection. In his soliloquy we glimpse the
soul of a man whose intellectual capacities, although in
the service of personal power rather than of the ideal
world, are on a level with Hamlet's own. Seeing retribution almost upon him, he makes a pitiful attempt to
recapture his original guiltlessness, to relate himself
again to the normative world, to conjure grace from
heaven, to achieve a reversal of divine justice. It is in
desperation that he turns to prayer. But he cannot pray
without repenting of his sin, and he cannot repent of it
while retaining its fruits. He is too far gone to return to
innocence.

My words fly up, my thoughts remain below.
Words without thoughts never to heaven go.

It is in the midst of the King's attempt at prayer,
as he kneels on the faldstool with his back turned, that
Hamlet passes by on his way to his mother's chamber.
He sees the King on his knees, unattended and unaware
of his presence. The occasion that will never recur
hangs, now, on the instant that will never return.
Hamlet draws his sword. . . . Then he pauses, sword in
hand, to tell himself that now he will do the deed of

vengeance. The pause is fatal. What he actually tells himself is that now he "might" do it. Telling himself what he might do, he sets off a dialogue with himself. What, he asks himself, would be the consequences of the doing ? —and by the time he has asked himself this the instant is gone, the King is out of danger.

The best comment on Hamlet's critical pause had already been made in his own third soliloquy:

> . . . the native hue of resolution
> Is sicklied o'er with the pale cast of thought,
> And enterprises of great pith and moment
> With this regard their currents turn awry,
> And lose the name of action.

Soliloquizing instead of acting, Hamlet now formulates a rationalization to which the King, himself, has just given the lie. Because the King is piously praying, he tells himself, he is in a state of holiness, and if he dies in such a state he will go to heaven instead of to the purgatory to which he had sent Hamlet's father by taking him "grossly, full of bread, with all his crimes broad blown." No, the vengeance to which he is pledged must await a better occasion. He recalls that, at this moment, he has another mission.

> My mother stays:
> This physic but prolongs thy sickly days.

Exit Hamlet.

20. <u>Forgive me this my virtue</u>.

Having turned away from confrontation with the King, Hamlet now turns to confront his mother. His relation to her, like his relation to Ophelia, is one of love and revulsion combined. According to his father's ghost (speaking only the thoughts of young Hamlet himself), lust was what had moved her to betray his

father's memory. In adjuring Hamlet to take vengeance it
had said:

> Let not the royal bed of Denmark be
> A couch for luxury and damned incest.

Hamlet was not, however, to take direct vengeance on
his mother as on his uncle:

> But, howsoever thou pursuest this act,
> Taint not thy mind, nor let thy soul contrive
> Against thy mother aught; leave her to heaven,
> And to those thorns that in her bosom lodge,
> To prick and sting her.

On his way, now, to confront his mother, Hamlet
reminds himself of what his bearing toward her must be:

> O heart ! lose not thy nature; let not ever
> The soul of Nero enter this firm bosom;
> Let me be cruel, not unnatural;
> I will speak daggers to her, but use none;
> My tongue and soul in this be hypocrites;
> How in my words soever she be shent,
> To give them seals never, my soul, consent !*

---

*   The reference to Nero may be apter than one might
suppose. The man Nero's mother took in second
marriage, like the man Hamlet's mother has taken in
second marriage, bore the name Claudius; and since
he was her uncle the marriage was incestuous, as
Hamlet considered his mother's second marriage to
be. Nero, the child of her first marriage, became
the stepson and heir of the Emperor Claudius just
as Hamlet, also the child of a first marriage, has
become the stepson and heir of King Claudius. In
the end, Nero killed his mother, and we see in
Hamlet the fear that he might do likewise. The
young Nero had been distinguished by his qualities
of soul and intellect, although in his final years he

While Hamlet is on his way to his mother's chamber, formulating in his mind the aggressive initiative he will take in dealing with her, Polonius, about to hide himself behind the arras, is advising her on the aggressive initiative that she should take with him:

> Look you lay home to him;
> Tell him his pranks have been too broad to
> bear with . . .
> Pray you, be round with him.

The Queen, like Ophelia, is always implicitly disposed to follow authority.

Because Hamlet and his mother each plan to accuse the other of misbehavior, their initial encounter produces an inevitable confusion. The power of Hamlet's verbal onslaught, however, quickly overcomes the Queen. As she turns in angry bewilderment to leave the room, he seizes her by the arm and forces her to sit down.

> You go not, till I set you up a glass
> Where you may see the inmost part of you.

Finding herself in the grip of a madman, as she takes him to be, she cries out for help, and Polonius in sudden alarm echoes her cry from behind the arras. Hamlet, now in headlong pursuit of his purpose, whirls and with one stroke plunges his sword through the arras. This time there has been no pause for thought, and this time, he believes, he has killed the King. But, as he lifts the arras, it is the body of the old courtier that tumbles to the floor. This is the first death of the play. It will, in itself, be followed by a train of mortal consequences.

---

gave rein to those inordinate passions on account of which it might have been better if his mother had never borne him. We should neither overlook this parallel, which includes what all men have in common, nor carry it too far.

Polonius's life was too slight a thing for his death to divert Hamlet from the confrontation with his mother in which he has already begun to release the frustration that has so long been tormenting him. The release cannot be choked off merely because an old busybody has, at a dangerous moment, stumbled across his path and been felled. In language that seems to go to the very source of all good and evil, Hamlet exposes to his mother the contrast between two worlds: the world of harmony and love that his father had represented, the world of power, corruption, and lust that his uncle represents. How, in the face of this contrast, could she have turned away from the one, and against it, to embrace the other ? His speech, as it develops, strips the Queen of all the pretenses behind which she had been sheltering herself even from self-knowledge—until in the end, with horrified eyes, she sees herself as she has become. There is terror and pity in her agony. The woman who had depended on Hamlet's father, and who had then depended on his uncle, now turns to him in moral anguish to show her how she may escape from the burden of an unbearable guilt.

It is true of the two women of the play that they must always belong to one man or another: to a father, to a husband, to a lover, or to a son. Gertrude, like Ophelia, had not been brought up to stand by herself. She experiences, now, the same need to return to a lost innocence that has just driven Claudius to attempt prayer. But he has been the prime mover in evil, the seducer, while her evil as the seduced has been secondary. She has never been more than the mirror of virtue or vice in the man to whom, at any particular time, she has belonged; and therefore, like a mirror, she is always capable of changing what she represents. The recognition of this has been implicit from the beginning in the ghost's speech, in Hamlet's thought.

To reinforce Hamlet in his purpose and his compassion, the ghost now appears to him again, although invisible to his mother. His mother, noting how he is distracted from his communication with her by a visitation of which she is unaware, sees in his incomprehensible behavior the expression of his momentarily forgotten madness. When the ghost goes, however, he tells her in plain terms, speaking to her now as his ally, that he is not in fact mad, adding:

> Mother, for love of grace,
> Lay not that flattering unction to your soul,
> That not your trespass but my madness speaks. . . .
> Repent what's past; avoid what is to come;
> And do not spread the compost on the weeds
> To make them ranker.

Then he stops, suddenly conscious of something questionable in his moralizing—and in an altered tone he says: "Forgive me this my virtue." He has perhaps sensed the danger of falling into the role of the Pharisee. In any case, a society that has given itself over to self-indulgence is bound to view any expression of virtue in its midst as the representation of an intolerable prigishness.

"O Hamlet!" cries the Queen, now utterly his, "thou hast cleft my heart in twain."

"What shall I do?" she asks. And her son, replying as if he had been her father-confessor, tells her to resist the seduction of the King, and to keep the confidence into which he has just taken her.

> Be thou assured [she says], if words be made of breath,
> And breath of life, I have no life to breathe
> What thou hast said to me.

Now that they are, by a sudden reversal, fellow conspirators against the King from whom he is rescuing her, he reminds her that by the King's command he must leave for England, adding that Rosencrantz and Guildenstern are surely charged with carrying out a plot against him. But they have no more weight with him than Polonius; it will be mere sport to turn the tables on them.

Hamlet's high inner tension, at the beginning of the scene, has once more been relaxed. His philosophical detachment has returned. Looking down, as he is about to leave, on the frail body that he must take with him, he comments:

> This counsellor
> Is now most still, most secret, and most grave,
> Who was in life a foolish prating knave.

Relations between Hamlet and his mother are once more what they had been before his uncle had practiced upon her. He bids her good-night, now, as if their mutual confidence and affection had never been disturbed.

Leaving her chamber, he drags behind him like a broken doll the remains of Polonius.

21. <u>Howe'er my haps, my joys were ne'er begun</u>.

Hamlet out of the way, the King enters, attended by Rosencrantz and Guildenstern, to be confronted with the news of Polonius's death, which the Queen prudently attributes to Hamlet's madness.

The King, who knows how far to believe in his madness, instantly grasps the import of this news: "It had been so with us had we been there."

He is as quick to grasp its political implications. He will be blamed for Polonius's death. If he charges Hamlet with it publicly, Hamlet is likely to reveal another murder, and to reveal it explicitly this time. The son of the old King has a potential claim on the allegiance of "the distracted multitude," who love him and who may already sense that something has gone wrong in the Kingdom.

The King, his moment of funk and introspection

over, is now all action and guile. Since Hamlet's madness is, he says, a threat to all, he must be packed off to England no later than sunrise. He gives his orders, makes his dispositions. Among the latter is a sealed letter that Rosencrantz and Guildenstern, accompanying the Prince to England, shall present to the English King, enjoining him to encompass Hamlet's death.

> Till I know 'tis done,
> Howe'er my haps, my joys were ne'er begun.

Like that other murderous usurper, Macbeth, he finds that, having realized his ambition, he cannot enter into its enjoyment until the one honorable man who knows the circumstances is dead.

22. But, come; for England!

Increasingly, as the action has advanced since the opening scene on the platform, the course of events has acquired its own direction and momentum. The human beings are carried along, their range of choice progressively diminished as decisions already taken cut off alternatives. We feel the inward relief with which Hamlet, for whom action is not natural, increasingly resigns himself, cultivating the philosophical detachment by which he rises superior to the circumstances that carry him along. He offers no resistance to his dispatch to England, and seems to have forgotten his commitment to avenge his father.

His detachment takes various forms. One is represented by the casualness with which he shrugs off catastrophe, as in the case of Polonius's death. Another by an increasingly ironical commentary on the course of events. Humor plays its role, which is to provide detachment from what would otherwise be intolerable.

When, now guarded by soldiers, Hamlet is brought before the King, he is asked to reveal the whereabouts of Polonius, whose body he has hidden.

"At supper," he replies shortly. And then:

> Not where he eats, but where he is eaten: a
> certain convocation of politic worms are e'en
> at him. Your worm is your only emperor for
> diet: we fat all creatures else to fat us, and
> we fat ourselves for maggots. . . . A man
> may fish with the worm that hath eat of a
> king, and eat of the fish that hath fed of
> that worm.

When the King asks what this means, he replies:
"Nothing, but to show you how a king may go a progress through the guts of a beggar."

The King tells Hamlet he must prepare himself to
leave for England immediately, half expecting that he will
offer objections.

"Good," says Hamlet.

> KING. So is it, if thou knews't our
> purposes.

> HAMLET. I see a cherub that sees them.
> But, come; for England.

23. <u>Witness this army of such mass and charge</u>
    <u>Led by a delicate and tender prince . . .</u>

It is only at this late stage that the man who will
inherit the Kingdom appears on the scene. In fact,
neither here nor elsewhere does he participate in the
action of the play itself. He is essentially a symbolic
figure waiting in the wings to restore order when the
tragedy shall have completed its course. His appearance
here is merely an extraneous interlude to the action.
He does not come onto the stage in his own right until

the end of the final scene, when he will come forward and take command, terminating the play.

Fortinbras, Prince of Norway, appears as what the Prince of Denmark should have been. He is the efficient as opposed to the contemplative man, doing without hesitation or uncertainty whatever is to be done. What is to be done is, in turn, determined by a traditional code of honor about which there could be no question in his unquestioning mind. We have heard of him in the first court scene, when he was represented as a military menace to Denmark. Here he is again for a moment, this time in person, attending to the job in hand, which is no more than the conquest of a worthless patch of ground held by the Polish King. With his army he stands at the frontier of Denmark, near the port from which Hamlet is about to embark. He gives his orders succintly, no syllable wasted:

> Go, captain, from me greet the Danish king;
> Tell him that, by his license, Fortinbras
> Claims the conveyance of a promised march
> Over his kingdom. You know the rendezvous.
> If that his majesty would aught with us,
> We shall express our duty in his eye,
> And let him know so.

In its way, this speech is perfect. By the momentary authority of its terms, which pose a contrast, it diminishes Hamlet.

Having given his command, Fortinbras moves on with his army as Hamlet arrives on the scene. The direct confrontation of opposites fails at this point, as in the final scene, by no more than a moment of time—by so little that the voice of Fortinbras almost remains for Hamlet's ear. The captain to whom the Norwegian Prince's instructions were addressed has not yet moved on, the Norwegian army is still marching by.

The captain, having answered Hamlet's questions regarding the army and its objective, departs. Hamlet, with food for thought, bids his attendants continue on their course, leaving him to catch up. Here, still within the gravitational field of the perfect prince, he has a moment of self-contempt, like Lancelot when he thinks of Galahad. Wishing himself like Fortinbras, he only points the contrast by philosophical musings of which Fortinbras would be incapable:

> What is a man,
> If his chief good and market of his time
> Be but to sleep and feed ? a beast, no more.
> Sure he that made us with such large discourse,
> Looking before and after, gave us not
> That capability and god-like reason
> To fust in us unused. Now, whether it be
> Bestial oblivion, or some craven scruple
> Of thinking too precisely on the event,
> A thought, which, quartered, hath but one part wisdom,
> And ever three parts coward, I do not know
> Why yet I live to say 'This thing's to do';
> Sith I have cause and will and strength and means
> To do't. Examples gross as earth exhort me:
> Witness this army of such mass and charge
> Led by a delicate and tender prince,
> Whose spirit with divine ambition puffed
> Makes mouths at the invisible event,
> Exposing what is mortal and unsure
> To all that fortune, death and danger dare,
> Even for an egg-shell. Rightly to be great
> Is not to stir without great argument,
> But greatly to find quarrel in a straw
> When honour's at the stake. How stand I then,
> That have a father killed, a mother stained,
> Excitements of my reason and my blood,
> And let all sleep while, to my shame, I see
> The imminent death of twenty thousand men,
> That, for a fantasy and trick of fame,
> Go to their graves like beds, fight for a plot
> Whereon the number cannot try the cause,
> Which is not tomb enough and continent
> To hide the slain ? O! from this time forth,
> My thoughts be bloody, or be nothing worth!

But it is no use. The final exhortation to himself, in succession to so many that have gone before, no longer carries conviction. He is Hamlet, not Fortinbras, and more purely Hamlet as his character realizes itself progressively under the stress of circumstances closing in upon him, until at last all inner conflict will have resolved itself away, leaving the pure spirit of one who had been born out of place and out of time.

24. Conscience and grace, to the profoundest pit !

In a lapse of weeks between scenes, now, Hamlet has sailed for England and been captured by pirates who have returned him to the Danish coast. Rosencrantz and Guildenstern have gone on to England, not knowing that Hamlet has substituted, for the message they had been carrying, a forgery calling for their own deaths.

Meanwhile, the death of Polonius has started a train of consequences. One is that Ophelia, having lost first Hamlet and now her father, suffers a mental breakdown. She comes before the King and Queen, pitiful in the delusions of her madness, murmuring broken phrases that have disturbing undertones. In addition to grief at her father's death, her words suggest suspicion of treachery. They also carry the implication, which we have already caught, that the relationship between her and Hamlet had been, if only in their thoughts, less than innocent.

Polonius's death has, in addition, contributed to a growing uneasiness in the Kingdom. The people, seeing what they obscurely sense to be a counterfeit majesty on the throne, have begun to be troubled. The new King has not dared to give occasion to their trouble by holding a state funeral for Polonius, whose death remains a public mystery. At the same time, Hamlet, the personi- fication of legitimacy, has left Denmark with unwonted abruptness. One can imagine how, in these circum- stances, rumours would spread, generating a vague fear that it is the wolf who now wears the shepherd's clothing. The words that Ophelia speaks in her madness make their contribution to a general doubt.

In France, Laertes, hearing that his father is mysteriously dead and hastily buried, posts back to Denmark wild for vengeance, ready to challenge a King who has put himself under suspicion by his secrecy and his failure to hold a proper funeral. Mutiny forms in his wake as he makes his way to the palace, so that he is at the head of a clamoring mob when he arrives and bursts into the chamber where the King stands to receive his charge.

Laertes provides another contrast to Hamlet, this one pointed by a certain similarity of circumstances: for he also has to avenge a father killed, and he is to be tormented by the spectacle of a sister undone. But Laertes is not, like Fortinbras, "a delicate and tender prince." He is a ruffian, and what passes for his code of honor is the code of street-gangs. Now in his anger he is like a charging bull, seeming dangerous but easily deflected by the skilled toreador. The King is in danger only for the instant it takes him to check the headlong rush. That instant passed, he proceeds to play Laertes with composure and confidence.

Laertes has been checked at the last moment and stands bewildered, uncertain about the circumstances of his father's death. Frustrated, like Hamlet in a situation not dissimilar, he unpacks his heart with words:

> How came he dead ? I'll not be juggled with.
> To hell allegiance ! vows, to the blackest devil !
> Conscience and grace, to the profoundest pit !
> I dare damnation.

No less than Fortinbras, Hamlet, or the King, Laertes has a personal style of his own. But it lacks refinement.

While the King is placating Laertes a letter comes from Hamlet, reporting that he is on his way back, unattended. It is typical of Hamlet that, in contempt of guile, he should in advance announce his return to the King whom he knows to be plotting his death. So the King learns that his device for getting rid of Hamlet has misfired—and here at hand is Laertes, whose avenging fury he has just succeeded in deflecting from himself to Hamlet as the author of his father's death and his sister's madness. On the instant, then, he devises a new scheme whereby a fencing match will be arranged between Laertes and Hamlet. Laertes will have a foil that, contrary to the practice when fencing for sport, has not been blunted. Hamlet, he observes:

> . . . being remiss,
> Most generous and free from all contriving,
> Will not peruse the foils; so that with ease
> Or with a little shuffling, you may choose
> A sword unbated, and, in a pass of practice
> Requite him for your father.

Laertes immediately proposes to poison the tip of his foil, and the King, not to risk failure a second time, undertakes to have a poisoned drink ready for Hamlet when he calls for refreshment. News of Ophelia's death by drowning comes at this moment to clinch Laertes's determination.

So the final scene of the drama is approached.

25. He hath borne me on his back a thousand times.

In preparation for the final scene, we are now lifted above the tumultuous circumstances of place and time to see the actors and events from far away.

To Laertes, a minute before, the madness of Ophelia had filled the field of vision, and the catastrophe of her death had been coextensive with eternity. Now, however, we are in a remote graveyard where two grave-diggers are practicing their tranquil employment.

The prospective tenant of the grave is nothing to them, a gentlewoman who has them sweating over their spades because she walked into a stream and drowned herself.

> FIRST GRAVE-DIGGER. Is she to be buried in Christian burial that wilfully seeks her own salvation ?

> SECOND. I tell thee she is; and therefore make her grave straight: the crowner hath sat on her, and finds it Christian burial.

> FIRST. How can that be, unless she drowned herself in her own defence ?

> SECOND. Why, 'tis found so.

> FIRST. It must be 'se offendendo'; it cannot be else. For here lies the point: if I drown myself wittingly it argues an act; and an act hath three branches; it is to act, to do, and to perform: argal, she drowned herself wittingly.

> SECOND. Nay, but hear you, goodman delver,—

> FIRST. Give me leave. Here lies the water; good: here stands the man; good: if the man go to this water, and drown himself, it is, will he, nill he, he goes; mark you that ? but if the water come to him, and drown him, he drowns not himself: argal, he that is not guilty of his own death shortens not his own life.

> SECOND. But is this law ?

> FIRST. Ay, marry, is't; crowner's quest law.

> SECOND. Will you ha' the truth on't ?

If this had not been a gentlewoman she should have been buried out o' Christian burial.

FIRST. Why, there thou sayest; and the more pity that great folk should have countenance in this world to drown or hang themselves more than their even Christian.

Hamlet passes by, now, on his way back to the court, accompanied by Horatio, who had gone to his encounter. The second grave-digger has taken himself off to fetch a stoup of liquor, and the first, left alone, is singing as he digs. Hamlet, now in his natural role as observer rather than actor, pauses with Horatio to appreciate the quality of the scene. The distant view of life, in which human beings appear like ants about a mound, is native to him, and he embraces the occasion.

The old fellow in the grave, singing away, throws up a skull and, with a tap of his spade, fixes it against the growing pile of dirt. Hamlet comments to Horatio:

That skull had a tongue in it, and could sing once; how the knave jowls it to the ground, as if it were Cain's jaw-bone, that did the first murder ! This might be the pate of a politician, which this ass now o'er-offices, one that would circumvent God, might it not ?. . . Or of a courtier, which could say, 'Good morrow, sweet lord ! How dost thou, good lord ?' This might be my Lord Such-a-one, that praised my Lord Such-a-one's horse, when he meant to beg it, might it not ?. . . and now my Lady Worm's; chapless, and knocked about the mazzard with a sexton's spade. . . .

He asks the old grave-digger whose grave it is he is digging, thereby setting off a humorous game of words with him. ("Mine, sir," is the prompt answer.) The grave, it transpires, is for no man—nor no woman either. It is for "one that was a woman, sir; but, rest her soul, she's dead." (Hamlet, unaware, saves the moment by not carrying his inquiry to the point of asking her name.) The old fellow continues a rambling patter over a variety of topics, among them the young Hamlet, "he that is mad, and sent into England," where his madness will not be noticed because there the men are as mad as he. Hamlet has occasion to see himself, too, as merely an item in the passing swarm, one whose skull may in its turn be buffeted by a spade.

A second skull has been tossed onto the pile and he has picked it up, turning it about in his hand.

Whose might this have been ?

The old man with the spade, who has over the years buried as many as he has dug up again, identifies it as that of the former King's jester, Yorick.

This comes home to Hamlet, evoking affectionate memories of the merry man who had romped with him as a child. "He hath borne me on his back a thousand times. . . . Here hung those lips that I have kissed I know not how oft." As he contemplates the framework of bone in his hand something approaching a godlike view of human existence forms in him. We are moving, constantly, toward the serenity of death in the final scene. . . .

26. This is I, Hamlet the Dane.

At this point, however, the wordly life in all its urgency returns, intruding on the peaceful landscape. In solemn procession, accompanying the open coffin of Ophelia, the King, the Queen, Laertes, a Doctor of Divinity, and a retinue of courtiers enter.

Hamlet is still abstracted. To him in his detachment the members of the procession are like characters in a pantomine: a King, a Queen, attendants. He observes them from on high, forgetting that this particular King has killed his father, that this particular Queen is his mother. What interests him in the pageant is that it represents only the truncated ceremonial reserved for the funerals of persons who have taken their own lives.

He draws Horatio into concealment, saying: "Couch we awhile and mark." Then, as the ceremonial unfolds he comments on it to Horatio much as he had commented to Ophelia on the play that he had had the actors from Wittenberg perform before the court. ("That is Laertes, a very noble youth: mark.")

There is an element of disturbance in what should be an affair of measured pomp and solemnity. Laertes, who has already had to accept the burial of his father without the rites that were his due, is beside himself at the Doctor of Divinity's insistence, now, that Ophelia is not entitled to the full rites of one who has parted this life in peace. As the coffin is lowered into the grave he cries out: "I tell thee, churlish priest, a ministering angel shall my sister be, when thou liest howling."

At the words "my sister" Hamlet starts. In his state of abstraction he had not even asked himself whose funeral it could be that the royalty of Denmark attended. Even now he is slow to grasp that it is Ophelia's, and that she is dead apparently by her own agency.

The ceremony goes on, the Queen scattering flowers over the coffin in the grave, at the same time that, unaware of the effect it is bound to have on Laertes, she says:

Farewell !
I hoped thou shouldst have been my Hamlet's wife;
I thought thy bride-bed to have decked, sweet maid,
And not have strewed thy grave.

This is too much for what remains of Laertes's composure. Apostrophizing Ophelia and shouting maledictions on "that cursed head whose wicked deed thy most ingenious sense deprived thee of," he leaps into the grave and demands to be buried with her.

Hamlet is like a sleeper waking up, confusedly connecting himself again with the hot and immediate life from which he had become separated. He steps forward, now, increasingly infected by Laertes's excitement. We have seen how, from the beginning, the display of noble passion or purpose without the adulteration of thought has, in every instance, touched a nerve of guilt within him. In every instance he has responded by trying to generate a like passion or purpose in himself. He had tried to do so in connection with the mission to avenge his father's murder that his father's spirit, speaking with passion from beyond the grave, had laid on him. He had been moved to the same effort by the emotion that the First Player had manifested over Hecuba's bereavement, and again by the spectacle of Fortinbras's thoughtless daring. Each time, however, his effort had resolved itself in nothing more than empty rantings. Now his nerve of guilt has been touched again, this time by the spontaneous explosion of anger and grief in Laertes.

Trying vainly to come back to life, trying once again to play the thoughtless role that is not his, he again overdoes it.

> What is he whose grief
> Bears such an emphasis ? whose phrase of sorrow
> Conjures the wandering stars, and makes them stand
> Like wonder-wounded hearers ? This is I,
> Hamlet the Dane.

He leaps into the grave with Laertes, challenging him to a contest in demonstrations of grief. They grapple and have to be parted.

Hamlet, the spasm over, reverts quickly to the fatalistic detachment into which he has been gravitating, and from which he will not again emerge:

> Hear you, sir [he says to Laertes];

What is the reason that you use me thus ?
I loved you ever: but it is no matter;
Let Hercules himself do what he may,
The cat will mew and dog will have his day.

27. The readiness is all.

Again there is a calm, in Hamlet's spirit and over the scene. Relaxed and at leisure, in the great hall of the castle at Elsinore, he is telling Horatio the circumstances in which he was moved to replace the letter calling for his death, which Rosencrantz and Guildenstern had borne, with one calling for their own. He is impressed by the providential nature of these circumstances, which suggest the existence of "a divinity that shapes our ends, rough-hew them how we will."

Contemplating the villainy of the King, he remarks:

Does it not, thinks't thee, stand me now upon—
He that hath killed my king and whored my mother,
Popped in between the election and my hopes,
Thrown out his angle for my proper life,
And with such cozenage—is't not perfect conscience
To quit him with this arm ? and is't not to be damned,
To let this canker of our nature come
In further evil ?

The question, asked dispassionately, is hardly more than academic now. In showing Hamlet's increasing detachment from the existential situation it represents the progressive change that has been taking place within him since the play began.

What immediately troubles his conscience now, he tells Horatio, is "that to Laertes I forgot myself; for, by the image of my cause, I see the portraiture of his." He is no longer as troubled by a failure to avenge with the sword as by a failure to show compassion.

At this point a comic interlude is introduced by the entrance of Osric, a little peacock of a courtier who affects the more fantastical fashions of the day in dress and speech. He has come as a messenger from the King, inviting Hamlet to match himself against Laertes with the foils, the King having already wagered on him in anticipation of his acceptance. He gets himself so wound up in his verbal flourishes, however, and he is so mercilessly interrupted by a mocking Hamlet, that he is almost unable to deliver his message at all. The purest comedy of the play comes just here, as we stand on the threshold of the tragic conclusion.

Hamlet, when he has had his game with the little lord, accepts the invitation in a resigned and passive spirit, telling him:

> Sir, I will walk here in the hall; if it please his majesty, 'tis the breathing time of day with me; let the foils be brought, the gentleman willing, and the king hold his purpose, I will win for him an I can; if not, I will gain nothing but my shame and the odd hits.

To a second messenger from the King he says that he is ready to play the match immediately.

Alone again with Horatio, he expresses his confidence of winning at the odds—but also the misgivings he feels, which amount to a premonition of his death. ". . .thou wouldst not think how ill all's here about my heart; but it is no matter."

Horatio protests: "If your mind dislike any thing, obey it; I will forestal their repair hither, and say you are not fit." To which Hamlet replies, in no uncertainty now that he is letting events command him:

> Not a whit, we defy augury; there's a special providence in the fall of a sparrow. If it be now, 'tis not to come; if it be not to

come, it will be now; if it be not now, yet it will come: the readiness is all.

And so:

> Attendants enter to set benches and carry in cushions for the spectators: next follow trumpeters and drummers with kettle-drums, the King, the Queen and all the court, Osric and another lord, as judges, bearing foils and daggers which are placed upon a table near the wall, and last of all Laertes dressed for the fence.

28. You that look pale and tremble at this chance . . .

Hamlet goes up to Laertes and takes his hand. This, in the final scene of the tragedy, is the loving and gracious Hamlet who had welcomed his school-mates and the players from Wittenberg:

> Give me your pardon, sir; I've done you wrong;
> But pardon't, as you are a gentleman.
> This presence knows, and you must needs have heard,
> How I am punished with a sore distraction.
> What I have done,
> That might your nature, honour and exception
> Roughly awake, I here proclaim was madness.
> . . . .
> Sir, in this audience,
> Let my disclaiming from a purposed evil
> Free me so far in your most generous thoughts,
> That I have shot mine arrow o'er the house,
> And hurt my brother.

They proceed to the choice of rapiers. Laertes is uneasy at the treachery he is about to practice upon one who has just dealt with him in such noble and concilia-ting terms. Therefore, when the match begins he finds himself inwardly inhibited in the use of the unbated and poisoned rapier that he holds in his hand. He fences half-heartedly, and Hamlet, with his blunted foil, scores the first two hits.

The King, seeing Laertes's hesitancy, has in an interval of rest urged Hamlet to refresh himself with the drink he has prepared for him; but Hamlet has put it aside. Now the Queen takes it up to drink to Hamlet's success, and before the King can stop her has swallowed the poison.

Laertes is inwardly rebellious at what seems an unmanly hesitation in himself to proceed with the plot for avenging his father's death. Suddenly, then, during another interval of rest, with Hamlet off guard, he lunges at him, wounding him slightly with the poisoned point. Hamlet, in a spontaneous reaction of angry surprise, leaps at him, they scuffle, the rapiers clatter to the ground, and when they pick them up again it is the poisoned rapier that Hamlet unknowingly holds. In the furious pass that follows, an aroused Hamlet wounds a confused and fearful Laertes.

Now the full dénouement is upon us. It is the last moment of the tragedy, when all the secret springs of action by which the actors had been brought to this pass are exposed to them. The Queen, sinking to the ground, cries out that the drink meant for Hamlet has poisoned her. A dying Laertes confesses to the treachery of the poisoned foil, begs Hamlet's forgiveness, and accuses the King. And now at last, with no further occasion for thought, when nothing more remains to be lost, Hamlet turns upon the King and carries out his vengeance.

The Queen, the King, and Laertes die in succession. Hamlet is left dying. "I am dead, Horatio," he says—and then, in the silence that follows:

> You that look pale and tremble at this chance,
> That are but mutes or audience to this act,
> Had I but time,—as this fell sergeant, death,

Is strict in his arrest,—O ! I could tell you—
But let it be. Horatio, I am dead;
Thou livest; report me and my cause aright
To the unsatisfied.

Horatio, now losing his head for perhaps the first time in his life, seizes the poisoned cup:

Never believe it [he cries];
I am more an antique Roman than a Dane:
Here's yet some liquor left.

But it is necessary, as Hamlet knows, that Horatio live—for the world will continue, there will be a new generation in government, and through all time to come successive generations of "mutes or audience." The individual is mortal, but the race is not. With a last spasm of strength, the dying Hamlet wrests the cup from Horatio's hand:

O God ! Horatio, what a wounded name,
Things standing thus unknown, shall live behind me.
If thou did'st ever hold me in thy heart,
Absent thee from felicity awhile,
And in this harsh world draw thy breath in pain,
To tell my story.

The tramp of soldiers marching is now heard, and the sound of a shot. The scene is interrupted. For a moment everything hangs suspended, no one moving. Then Osric goes out to investigate and returns to report the simultaneous arrival of the ambassadors from England (who bear the message, now inconsequential, that Rosencrantz and Guildenstern have been put to death) and of Fortinbras returning from conquest in Poland.

Hamlet, who still in the moment of death has the widest vision of time and the world, still looks to the future:

O ! I die, Horatio;
The potent poison quite o'er-crows my spirit:

I cannot live to hear the news from England,
But I do prophesy the election lights
On Fortinbras: he has my dying voice;
So tell him, with the occurents, more and less,
Which have solicited— The rest is silence.

29. Take up the bodies.

    The tragedy is over. But the world must be begun again, the dead must be buried, government and order must be re-established, provision must be made for the continuing business of life as a new generation assumes the burden. Amid the silence of death, the sound of the drum is heard, distant and then nearer. Fortinbras and his retinue enter.

    Only the poor student, Horatio, remains to be the intermediary between past and future. It is he who, as Hamlet has provided, is to hand over the keys of the Kingdom. To Fortinbras he says now:

          Give order that these bodies
High on a stage be placed to the view;
And let me speak to the yet unknowing world
How these things came about. . . .

    Fortinbras assumes the command that is native to him. He turns to Horatio and says: "Let us haste to hear it, and call the noblest to the audience." Then, to the living remnants of the past before him:

    For me, with sorrow I embrace my fortune;
I have some rights of memory in this kingdom,
Which now to claim my vantage doth invite me.

Again he wastes neither the occasion nor words; yet he carries all off with the dignity of one who was born to rule. Dispassionately, he speaks the last words of the play now, a speech of formal phrases appropriate to the solemnity of death:

                              Let four captains
        Bear Hamlet, like a soldier, to the stage;
        For he was likely, had he been put on,
        To have proved most royally: and, for his passage,
        The soldiers' music and the rites of war
        Speak loudly for him.
        Take up the bodies: such a sight as this
        Becomes the field, but here shows much amiss.
        Go, bid the soldiers shoot.

The soldiers bear away the bodies, the while a dead march
is heard; after the which a peal of ordnance is shot off.

        The great matters that we have witnessed are al-
ready history.

———————————————————

III. THE WORLD AND HAMLET

1. The World

Hamlet lives in the world we all know, the world of corruption satirized in Voltaire's Candide, the world epitomized in Hans Christian Andersen's story, The Emperor's New Clothes. The corruption consists of the pretences of those who constitute society, whether at a Renaissance court or in the fashionable circles of our cities today.

Especially in the competitive upper ranges of society, the positions that people take on the issues that confront them, the attitudes they strike, are based, not on a concern for what is true, but on the objective of gaining credit for "right thinking." In an elementary form this can be observed among young intellectuals in the lobbies of any concert-hall after a symphonic performance. Each in his comment tries to give an impression of critical appreciation, using a fashionable vocabulary to show that he is one of the initiated. A Candide, listening to them, would be impressed by all the things they said they had heard in the music that had escaped him.

I recall an occasion when a famous orchestra performed a symphony by an avant-garde composer. I knew a number of its members and, seeing them regularly, used to check personal impressions with them after performances. At the performance in question I had, myself, heard only a chaos of sounds and isolated phrases. But the applause had been tumultuous, acquaintances of mine had claimed to find significance in the composition, and the newspaper critics had discussed

83

it with respect. Later, one of the instrumentalists confided to me that conductor and orchestra alike had treated it as a joke. For example, he said, in one movement the woodwind section had abandoned all pretence of following the score: one member had embarked on Frère-Jacques, whereupon the others had taken it up; another had then started them on Sur le pont d'Avignon; and so forth. The critics who had discussed the fine points of the composition and its performance in abstruse terms had not dared allow themselves to recognize that the emperor was naked, for fear (as the tale puts it) of being considered unfit for their jobs.

Another example comes from The New York Times (International Edition) of August 2, 1961, which reported a joke that members of the British Broadcasting Company's music division played on their listeners. They claimed to be presenting a performance of a work called "Mobile for Tape and Percussion" by a Polish composer for whom they invented the name "Piotr Zak." What they actually did was disclosed by Susan Bradshaw of the music division. "We dragged together all the instruments we could find," she said, "and went around the studio banging them." The next day the London Times carried a serious analysis of the composition by its music critic, who was not going to show himself unfit for his job.

I have mentioned music critics, but they are not the only specialists in the clothing of emperors. I recall how shocked I was, when myself still a child, to read in Edward Bok's autobiography that, as drama critic for a New York newspaper, he sometimes did not bother to attend the performances of which he wrote his criticisms, relying on his native ingenuity to carry off the bluff. Most book-reviewers rarely do more than sample the books they review. They depend on a kind of bluff that becomes second nature to them, adopting a style of magisterial authority and indulging in little tricks of allusion and citation to suggest their mastery of the book's subject.

This universal pretence is no less prevalent in the

councils of government, where the current fashion in right thinking quite overrides truth. It was no less prevalent in Renaissance courts such as the one Shakespeare was representing in <u>Hamlet</u>.

In this corrupt world, anyone who seeks to emulate the child of the Andersen tale, and to make his career on that basis, will find himself facing barriers that are all but insurmountable. He will find himself intellectually isolated, standing in opposition to the common mind that governs the society in which he is trying to make his career. He will find that he has aroused, among the insiders who represent the common mind, the same atavistic instinct of hostility toward the outsider that is in evidence on any school playground.

The first barrier that he must face is that of confidence in his own faculties; for few of us have the self-assurance to believe even in the simple testimony of our own eyes when everyone around us is admiring the emperor's new clothes. Many of us who have sat at the council-tables of government have had the experience of not daring to speak up when everyone else agreed on what appeared to be plainly untrue, fearing that we had missed some essential point in the argument or overlooked some factor evident to all the others—fearing that we would show ourselves unfit for our jobs.

The second barrier is in the power of those who represent the common mind to deny the outsider advancement in his career and opportunities for publication, or to discredit his work if it appears as a book for review. Where the standards of book-reviewing are pragmatic rather than principled, the first question to present itself to a reviewer is whether the author is "one of us," and on the basis of the answer he decides whether the author should be honored or discredited. Some months after an unfavorable review of my first book had appeared I met the reviewer for the first time and we came to know each other. One day he told me, as if it had long been bothering him, that of course if he had known me when he had reviewed my book he would have reviewed it favorably. What apparently had been weighing on his conscience had nothing to do with the merits of the book itself.

Again, if the man who thinks for himself wants a university appointment or hopes for promotion he is likely to find the way barred by those who represent the common academic mind.

A mitigating element in our open societies is that there is no official establishment of state or church to enforce unity of belief, with the result that a range of diversity, manifesting itself in rival schools of thought, rival establishments, exists. Certain attitudes and conceptions may, at any given time, have absolute sway, but otherwise there may be variety and conflict among competing groups. The individual who normally could not survive in isolation is thereby afforded at least some choice among rival establishments, each with its own common mind. The corruption remains, however, since it is only the independant individual, thinking for himself alone, free to follow wherever the argument may lead, who can devote himself without compromise to the pursuit of truth.

The pretences to which I have referred are related to the process of forming the collective mind. The individual, as one member of a group that has to formulate its collective opinions on the issues to which it addresses itself, is involved in the politics of negotiation and compromise at the level of the common mind, which is never high. In these circumstances, the question is never one of truth but of what attitudes to strike; and the question of what attitudes to strike is a question of what will best promote the group's power in society, a power with which its members have identified themselves. This is what comes to constitute right thinking.

We take this kind of thing for granted in the behavior of political parties, but it has hardly been less true of French painters for generations past. Each has had to belong to a school with the equivalent of a political platform. Each has had to be a Fauve or a Cubist, an Expressionist, a Dadaist, or a Surrealist. Each, having to represent the right thinking of a particular establishment, has been the less free to cultivate and to paint his individual vision. Painting has, in fact, been extraordinarly like politics, a matter of 'isms, manifestos, and collective action.

Literary intellectuals, for their part, have belonged to categorically defined and recognized ideological groupings. This has taken away any loneliness that might otherwise have accompanied the "alienation" they have proclaimed, for it has associated them with one another in the bond of a common intellectual fashion. To their groupings they have given their allegiance. ("La gauche," said a leading French intellectual, "c'est une patrie.") To the glorification of their groupings they have dedicated themselves in language of the highest altruism. ("The writer," wrote a writer, "is the conscience of the world.") On their groupings they have depended for their intellectual security and the security of their careers. And the only sacrifice that security has exacted is the pursuit of truth.

The same inescapable corruption pervades all professional and vocational circles. We take for granted the shoe-manufacturer's conviction that the general interests of society require a protective tariff against foreign shoes. But Plato, himself, was sure that philosophers should be kings. Anyone who suggests to a gathering of physical scientists that the world might not be better off if it were run only by people with their training and discipline will get a cold reception. Anyone who suggests to political scientists that they are not qualified, as such, to take over the decision-making functions of government will find that they regard him as unsound. There will be pursed lips and a shaking of heads.

Is this not the world of <u>Candide</u> ?

In all academic communities a distinction may be made between what everyone says and what is true. The

87

former is, in a word, "correct." Students at examinations, or in the papers they submit, may be well advised to aim at "correct" answers. The training they are undergoing is primarily in the orthodoxy that such answers represent. Again, wherever an ideological establishment rules the only question that arises is that of what is "correct," and the very word "truth" disappears. So a sort of scholastic formalism develops that corrupts the intellectual enterprise of mankind. It has been so in all ages, in our own no less than in Galileo's.

The barriers to survival, in his career, of an individual who thinks for himself are not necessarily insurmountable. In exceptional circumstances, involving luck or the special providence referred to by Hamlet, he may at least be able to keep going for the normal duration of his career. But the barriers are so formidable and intimidating that, in all but extraordinary cases, there can be no question of not respecting them.

Every society is in constant danger of being finally overcome by the corruption I have described. That is why every society needs, in addition to the orthodox establishments that give it stability, a Socrates or a Voltaire for its constant purgation. I am not sure, however, that a Socrates or a Voltaire would have much chance of surviving in the highly organized mass-societies of our day, unless briefly and by virtue of an exceptional combination of circumstances. In a simpler age, Socrates did not need a publisher, a lecture-platform, an academic stipend, funds to support his studies; and although the difficulties and dangers that confronted Voltaire were in some respects even greater than those that would confront him today, they are different difficulties and dangers.

I derive encouragement, however, from the fact that in our own day we do have one man who, although governed by the Socratic compulsion, has somehow survived. Milovan Djilas, in a country under an ideological dictatorship, has thought for himself and has been moved to utter, at all hazards, what he has thought. But it is only a combination of extraordinary personal circumstances that has allowed him to survive, albeit in jail for many years, and the publishers he has found have been in countries hostile to the official ideology, to which he has had to smuggle what he wrote. It would be hard to contemplate the future of mankind if the possibility of a Socrates or a Djilas in our midst were finally foreclosed.

+ + +

What I have attempted to show above is the corruption that prevails at all the levels of power and influence in our world of today, as in ancient Greece, in Rome, in Medieval and in Renaissance Europe, in ancient Persia, in Bysantium, in Confucian and in Communist China. This corruption is always tending to engulf us, to become total. The saving grace, time and again, is that of the incorruptible individual who thinks for himself, is under an inner compulsion to utter what he thinks, and still survives long enough to be heard.

The corruption is especially conspicuous at the seat of government, where the competition for place and power is generally so fierce as to break down, repeatedly, the ordinary ethical barriers that limit human relations in civilized societies. In Washington or White-hall, as must be even more the case in Moscow or Peking, all the devices of conspiracy are used, on occasion, to destroy rivals; and the degree of progress in civilization is exemplified only by abstinence from such measures of physical violence as continue to be practiced in Latin America, in Africa, and in parts of Asia—as were practised in Hamlet's Denmark. Government still, however, is essentially conspiracy. Therefore, men like Thomas More and Milovan Djilas can survive in it for a time only, and then only by virtue of the extraordinary circumstances that we know. For the most part, a Socrates or a Voltaire will avoid it. Hamlet, to his sorrow, was born into it, and the obligations imposed on him by his father's death, in addition to the general obligations of his heritage, foreclosed any possibility of escape that he might otherwise have found. His return to his studies at Wittenberg was forbidden him. There is poignance, then, in his exclamation:

> The time is out of joint; O cursed spite
> That ever I was born to set it right !

2. Hamlet

Hamlet stands alone in opposition to his environment, unable to adjust himself to the existential world of corruption, unable to make the convenient thinking of others his own. His mind is dominated by a normative model of the world, a conception of what it was intended to be. He happens to identify this world with his father, with the legitimacy that his father's reign had represented, and with the legitimacy that his father's marriage to his mother had represented. He finds himself living, however, in the world as it is, and the contrast that it makes with the legitimate world of his mind induces in him a revulsion against it.

Now this is common enough experience, known in some degree to all who have ever given their allegiance to a normative model of the world. Two alternative responses are possible. One is to address oneself to the task of reforming the corrupt existential world; the other is simply to withdraw. Withdrawal may be achieved, in its degree, by entering a monastery (where, however, the corruption will not be altogether absent), by retiring to a contemplative life of some sort, or simply by retreating into one's own mind and abstaining from the corrupting competition of the market-place. In Hamlet's case an array of special circumstances militates against withdrawal. He has been born into a position that, in spite of the primitive elective system still prevailing, makes him, at least implicitly, heir apparent to the Danish throne. In this respect his position is not unlike that of King Edward VIII of Britain, who finally abdicated in 1936.

For he himself is subject to his birth;
He may not, as unvalued persons do,
Carve for himself, for on his choice depends
The safety and the health of the whole state;
And therefore must his choice be circumscribed . . .

The constitutional obstacle to withdrawal is not in itself insurmountable, but in Hamlet's case it is decisively reinforced by the filial obligation to avenge his father and redeem the Kingdom. He finds himself under a moral obligation, regarded as sacred, to reform the world rather than withdraw from it.

The basic conflict, then, is between Hamlet's nature, which is that of a detached contemplative, and the inescapable obligations of his position, which call for a man of action.

We may well ask what an able man of action, a Fortinbras, would have done in Hamlet's position. It is not plausible that he would simply have waylaid the King and cut him down without considering the consequences and preparing for them. (Perhaps a Laertes would have done this, as Jack Ruby cut down the supposed assassin of President Kennedy, but not a Fortinbras.) Presumably, if he had done this he could have expected to be killed by the King's men in return, and so the Kingdom would have been left in disarray, without a head. He would therefore have made arrangements for assuming the crown himself, as the ranking lord of the Kingdom, immediately upon his uncle's removal. This would, however, have required him to organize in advance, and secretly, a conspiracy involving a number of people to carry out a coup d'état. He would initially have had to work with confidants like Horatio, cautiously enlarging the circle as opportunity offered, just as Cassius organized the stroke against Caesar. Together they would have had to exploit such dissatisfaction as was to be found in the Kingdom in order to build up a following, and that in secrecy. There would have had to be a coordination of moves, signals arranged in advance, a time-table of action, etc.

Undoubtedly Denmark was full of men who had a natural aptitude for this sort of thing and would have had fair chances of success in carrying it off. It was, however, altogether contrary to Hamlet's nature, and in fact he never even considered undertaking it. All he considered, under the stress of an accusing conscience, was to find an occasion for running his sword through the King, and this was an impractical and therefore unreal approach. When he found the King alone at prayers he was right to refrain from killing him on the spot, but not for the reason he invented to justify his inaction.

Polonius had concluded the string of precepts with which he speeded Laertes, upon his departure for France, with:

> To thine own self be true,
> And it must follow, as the night the day,
> Thou canst not then be false to any man.

Hamlet was torn between being true to his own nature and being true to the obligations of his birth:

> The time is out of joint; O cursed spite,
> That ever I was born to set it right !

(The emphasis is on the "I.") In the end he remained true to himself—and this was inevitable, since no man can ultimately escape being what he is.

The paradox of Hamlet's position was that, to realize the normative world in action, he would have had to embrace all the sordid devices of the existential world. He would have had to practice corruption to overcome corruption. He would have had to adopt the pragmatic means of conspiracy: secrecy, double dealing, hypocrisy, and violence. He would have had to give himself entirely to the struggle for personal power, thereby corrupting himself—so that he might indeed have ended as Nero did.

It is a standard dilemma of the world that has followed the expulsion from Paradise that one can hold to one's ideals, avoiding their betrayal in practice, only by withdrawal, by refusal to participate. Hamlet, moved by a revulsion against the corruption of the existential world, was consequently inhibited from embracing its devices even in the name of ushering in the ideal world.

Was this weakness ?

Surely it was. I myself, living in a pragmatic post-paradisial world, have had to discipline myself all my life to acknowledge what is required to keep the world going, to maintain its essential functioning from year to year, from generation to generation—what is required simply to ward off chaos. I have had to discipline myself to reject the idealist's contempt for workability (for what he sometimes calls "expediency"), which he can maintain only so long as he, himself, remains aloof from direct responsibility for keeping the world going. I also have lived a good part of my life in the society of practical men who have not flinched from the terrible burdens of public responsibility, or from the requirements that go with them. In principle, then, I can recognize Hamlet's misfortune in being born to such responsibility, but I cannot quite allow myself to commend him for his refusal to accept it. On the face of it, such a refusal is indeed weakness, and the weakness it represents is the cause of the tragedy that the play enacts, just as the weakness of Macbeth is the cause of the tragedy that <u>Macbeth</u> enacts, just as the weakness of Lear and Othello are the causes of the respective tragedies that <u>King Lear</u> and <u>Othello</u> enact.

If, however, the question is not one of approval but of sympathy, then I must acknowledge myself on Hamlet's side. I, myself, have been increasingly free, as he was not, to follow Polonius's precept, and I have never had the slightest compunction at withdrawing, in the second half of my life, just as far as circumstances allowed me to. I have felt binding obligations to my family (which would, for example, rule out withdrawal to a monastery, like Santayana, or indulgence in such a life as was led by Socrates), but I have felt no obligation at all to act on the assumption that I was qualified, morally or otherwise, to undertake the reform of the world.

No, the tragedy was inevitable. Even if Hamlet had set himself to carry out his role as Prince of Denmark, trying to be another Fortinbras, he would have failed, just as I would have failed if I had found myself Prime Minister of Britain in World War II and had tried to be another Churchill.

I question, moreover, whether the pure man of action represents the highest type of mankind. To me, the glory of our species is the human mind at the extremes of self-conscious awareness represented by a Socrates, a Montaigne, a Pascal, a Shakespeare—or a Hamlet. To me Voltaire represents a higher type than Napoleon, and much as I admire Pericles I would set Thucydides above him. This is to say that I set Hamlet above Fortinbras, although it would have been better if Fortinbras had been born Prince of Denmark. It is not that mankind does not depend alike on its Fortinbras and its Hamlets; but it depends on the former for its present salvation, on the latter for its ultimate salvation. We must save the world from day-to-day, and for that we need our Fortinbras; but if we are ever to emerge from the tragic dilemmas of this post-paradisial age it will only be by that constant enlargement of our under-standing for which we depend on the few thoughtful, introspective, and incorruptible minds that are able to work in something approaching the ideal of academic detachment. Hamlet's personal tragedy was that this, his true vocation, was denied him by inescapable circum-stances.

3.   Death

The pure man of action does not, ordinarily, allow his mind to dwell on the approach of death. When ad-

vancing years and the progressive impairment of his
faculties do, at last, force him to think of it, he
anticipates it with horror and hopes that he can continue
to keep it far from the real present in which he still
lives his life of action.

In all contemplative persons, by contrast, there is
likely to be something like a love of death that develops
as they grow older. I do not mean that they are in a
hurry to end their lives. It is merely that they find
solace in the thought:

> That no man lives forever,
> That dead men rise up never;
> That even the weariest river
> Winds somewhere safe to sea.

To one who does not find himself at home in the
existential world his own passage through it may seem
like that of a man crossing a chasm on a tightrope.
Especially in youth, with his career ahead of him, he
may doubt that he can ever make it to the other side;
but he finds himself committed simply by the astonishing
circumstance that here he is, having in his first
consciousness found his feet already on the rope and the
chasm open beneath him. As the years of his life pass,
then, as his career takes its direction and lengthens
out, he may feel an increasing self-confidence. Now he
is halfway across the chasm, now two-thirds across,
within sight of the end—and now he feels some
assurance that he can make it all the way. Having
already gone so far, he has become experienced, he has
acquired a knack, and he looks back with a certain pity
at his first awkward steps in a past that has come to
seem remote. At the same time, however, he is conscious
of how the strain continues, never allowing him to relax
from effort; he is conscious of continuing fear, based on
the continuing danger exemplified by so many others
who, at every stage of the crossing, fall into unexpected
disaster; and he feels increasingly the weariness that
accumulates in one's bones as one goes on through so
many decades. Under the circumstances, the farther

shore begins to seem like a haven. Here at last is the end of striving and the end of fear. Here at last is perfect sleep. When he thinks that this sleep may well be one from which he will never awaken he may be glad that it is not already upon him—but since it must come anyway, if not sooner then later, he is not offered a choice. The option of living and suffering forever in this existential world, with never any rest, never any surcease from anxiety, with griefs and disasters succeeding one another through all eternity—this option, which might well be regarded as intolerable, does not present itself for his consideration. Either he will realise the full design, completing his life at the farther shore, or he will fall into the chasm before he gets there; and in either case there will be the same finality of eternal oblivion, if that is what death represents.

Throughout my adult life I have been peculiarly moved by contemplation of the life cycle, and by the logical relationship between that cycle and the survival of the species. The mortality of the individual and the immortality of the kind, renewed by each mortal generation, complement each other as parts of one design. The cycle of birth, of growing up, of maturity, of decline, and of death—this has its own harmony and symmetry. It is the ideal design established by God or nature. It is the Logos. Like Pythagoras contemplating the rhythmic order of the spheres, I find in it an unuttered music: it has the same quality of rhythm and regularity, the same logic. It satisfies in the same way. I feel as if I am, myself, playing my part in the great pageant of being: performing the life cycle in my own person, marrying, raising children to live after me, ending in completion when my time comes, leaving the succeeding generations to carry on in their turn through the same cycle, toward whatever may be the ultimate end of mankind. This is not mysticism but rationalism: it is the apprehension of an a priori logic in the universe.

If one conceives of one's life in these terms, then one will wish to see one's part through to the end, one will wish to complete the cycle. But one will wish not to go beyond it; and one may still look forward to the end. One may still be in love with death.

This love of death is elemental in Hamlet, and it grows with his increasing maturity under the stress of circumstances. Death is constantly in his thoughts, but at first only as an escape from desperation, as when he exclaims in his first soliloquy:

> O ! that this too too solid flesh would melt,
> Thaw and resolve itself into a dew;
> Or that the Everlasting had not fixed
> His canon 'gainst self-slaughter !

This does not ring true. It is as rhetorical as it is real, a verbal release for frustration.

The case is different when, in the first scene of the third act, he confronts the full dilemma inherent in the obligation to avenge his father's death.

> To die: to sleep;
> No more; and, by a sleep to say we end
> The heart-ache and the thousand natural shocks
> That flesh is heir to, 'tis a consummation
> Devoutly to be wished.

It is a consummation, however, from which he still shrinks.

This first real expression of a longing for death is followed by the scene of the play within the play; and now we feel that the movement of the plot has passed a peak, that what remains is a process of resolution declining toward the finality of the end. In this declension, Hamlet is no longer struggling against the movement of events, or if he is so still it is only in occasional spasms of a troubled conscience. His acceptance of death is, in fact, what accounts for the marked change we see in him upon his return from England, when he stops to contemplate the spectacle of the grave-digger singing at his work. Already he is half in love with death as he muses over the skulls that the goodman delver tosses up with his spade. Death, as he here contemplates it, reduces the successes and failures of life to indifference: "Now get you to my lady's chamber, and tell her, let her paint an inch thick, to this favour she must come." Again, he asks: "Why may not imagination trace the noble dust of Alexander, till he find it stopping a bung-hole ?"

> Imperious Caesar, dead and turned to clay,
> Might stop a hole to keep the wind away.

Eventually, in his increasingly objective vision, he and the usurping King and all will be reduced to skulls like these, "chapless, and knocked about the mazzard with a sexton's spade." He had already been developing this consoling point of view when, on the eve of his departure for England, he had undertaken to show the horrified King "how a king may go a progress through the guts of a beggar."

At last, when death is no longer more than minutes away, his feelings are almost but not quite unmixed. There is still, as there must be, a note of regret and misgiving. ("Thou wouldst not think how ill all's here about my heart.") It is only a note, however, lacking the mortal anguish of which his earlier self had been capable, when he had repeatedly confronted the prospect of death only to turn away from it. Now he can console himself that "there's a special providence in the fall of a sparrow." In his last words to Horatio, as he lies dying, he calls upon him not to join him in death for the time being but, rather, to absent himself from "felicity" a while. By contrast with his agony of spirit in the first half of the play, the serenity that goes with this acceptance of death constitutes a happy ending to tragedy.

> Fear no more the frown o' the great,
>   Thou art past the tyrant's stroke:
> Care no more to clothe and eat;
>   To thee the reed is as the oak:

The sceptre, learning, physic, must
All follow this, and come to dust.

4. Socrates

The same detachment and acceptance of death marks
the last days of Socrates, as reported in Plato's Apology,
Crito, and Phaedo. It is only at the end of his life that
we know Socrates at all, when he has completed his
three score years and ten. At such an age he has
already crossed the chasm and is at the farther shore.
If he should still go on living indefinitely, marking time
as old men do, he could expect little but increasing
decay. This is the proper time for him to die, and if he
has any misgivings, as he advances to his death, he
hardly lets them show.

We may well doubt, however, that Socrates has
always been as we see him in his full age. He has
already survived seven decades of tumult and chaos, the
best and the worst in the history of Athens; and he has
survived by learning to detach himself in his own mind,
by cultivating an inner life of his own in contempt of his
existential environment. He, himself, has been under
savage attack, as we see in the ridicule that Aristophanes heaped on him in The Clouds at a time when he
was still only forty-seven years old. He had learned to
take these things in his stride, as every philosopher
supposedly should, and perhaps he had long ago come to
constitute an exception to Leonato's dictum that "there
was never yet philosopher that could endure the tooth-
ache patiently." (He had made a name for himself by his
indifference to creature comforts, and it was told how,
when discharging his compulsory military service in the
Thracian winter, he had appeared unaffected by
extremes of cold, walking about in ordinary clothes and
barefoot on the ice.)

Socrates, in his maturity, was moved by a compul-

99

sion to be true to himself that required him to persist in a line of questioning which was bound to expose the falsity of those intellectual attitudes, conceptions, and formulations that were held by the common mind of his day—although this was not his objective. Almost in spite of himself, he exposed the pretences of the ruling intellectuals, which presumably were not different in kind from the pretences of the ruling intellectuals of our own day. Explaining, in his defence before the Athenian Assembly, why he was the object of such widespread hostility, he told how, on one occasion:

> I went to one who had the reputation of wisdom. . . . When I began to talk with him, I could not help thinking that he was not really wise, although he was thought wise by many, and still wiser by himself; and thereupon I tried to explain to him that he thought himself wise, but was not really wise; and the consequence was that he hated me, and his enmity was shared by several who were present and heard me. . . . Then I went to one man after another, becoming conscious of the enmity which I provoked, and it distressed and alarmed me: but necessity was laid upon me.

The conclusion at which he finally arrived (and surely it would be true in our day as well) was "that the men most in repute were all but the most foolish; and that others less esteemed were really wiser and better." Can one say in all honesty that the famous philosophers of the Oxford and Cambridge establishments, in the mid-twentieth century, were the wisest men in Britain ? Could one say that the record of the life of Mr. Jean-Paul Sartre showed him to have been the wisest man in France ? Could one say that Professor Martin Heidegger had shown himself to be the wisest in Germany ?

Socrates could hardly have practiced such intellectual independance if he had had to compete for university appointments, to appeal to the academic establishment for a lecture-platform, or to solicit publication by university presses. Nor could he have practiced it if he had been born heir to Pericles, with a sacred obligation laid upon him to liberate Athens from Cleon. To the men of Athens, before whom he was making his defence, he said:

> Do not be offended at my telling you the truth: for the truth is, that no man who opposes you or any other crowd and tries to prevent the many unjust and illegal acts which are done in the state, will save his life; he who will fight for the right, if he would live even for a brief space, must have a private station and not a public one.

Hamlet, on the eve of his death, consoles himself and Horatio that there is a special providence in the fall of a sparrow; but, as we see in his third soliloquy, he is really an agnostic whose wisdom consists in the knowledge of his own ignorance. In Phaedo Socrates, on the eve of his own death, consoles himself and his disciples with an account of the life-after-death to which he looks forward. But he, too, is an agnostic who knows only his own ignorance, and his allegiance to truth is, in the end, more important than his own spiritual comfort or the consolation of those he will leave behind. So, having given his account, he warns them against any uncritical acceptance of it:

> For at this moment I am sensible that I have not the temper of a philosopher; like the uneducated, I am only a partisan. Now the partisan, when he is engaged in a dispute, cares nothing about the rights of the question, but is anxious only to convince his hearers of his own assertions. And the difference between him and me at the present moment is merely this—that whereas he seeks to convince his hearers that what he says is true, I am rather seeking to convince myself; to convince my hearers is a

secondary matter with me. You see how selfish I am ! For if what I say is true, then I do well to be persuaded of the truth; but if there is nothing after death, still, during the short time that remains, I shall not distress my friends with lamentations, and my ignorance will not last, but will die with me, and therefore no harm will be done. This is the state of mind, Simmias and Cebes, in which I approach the argument. And I would ask you to be thinking of the truth and not of Socrates.

In the end Socrates, like Hamlet, is more than half in love with death. At his trial he rejects any possible alternative, although there can be no doubt that the jurors would have voted exile rather than death if he had been willing to ask for it. The Athenians, in fact, did not want to put him to death, and during the month of his imprisonment before the death-sentence could be carried out he was given the opportunity to escape. There was a general readiness to wink at such an escape, and Crito urged it on him in anguished terms. It is hard to read, in <u>Crito</u>, the strained arguments that Socrates offers in reply without believing that, in truth, the attraction of death had become such for him that he would not be denied it. He was seventy years old, he had reached the opposite shore, he had completed his mission.

There is about the final scene of <u>Phaedo</u>, in which he drinks the hemlock, the serenity that is implicit in the close of Hamlet's life. Ostensibly, Socrates has been defeated by his social environment, as Ahab is defeated by the white whale in the final scene of <u>Moby Dick</u>. But in truth it is he who has triumphed over the environment.

Plato, in publishing his <u>Apology</u>, saw to it that Socrates was vindicated in the eyes of posterity. With his dying breath Hamlet asks Horatio to perform the same service:

O God ! Horatio, what a wounded name,
Things standing thus unknown, shall live behind me.
If thou didst ever hold me in thy heart,
Absent thee from felicity awhile,
And in this harsh world draw thy breath in pain,
To tell my story.

We shall see below what the implications of this are. For
Hamlet is, in a sense, Shakespeare's own Apologia pro
Vita sua.

5. Thomas More

The life of Thomas More, for a time the principal
figure at the increasingly corrupt court of Henry VIII,
is in its circumstances closer to Hamlet's life. The
description that Robert Whittington gave of More in 1520,
fifteen years before his death, might be a description of
Hamlet: "More is a man of an angel's wit and singular
learning. . . . And, as time requireth, a man of
marvellous mirth and pastimes, and sometime of as sad
gravity. A man for all seasons."

He was brought up in the household of Henry VII's
Lord Chancellor, so that he was familiar with politics and
court life from the earliest age. He had a scholarly bent
and, from the time he went to Oxford as a student, was
closely associated with those who were promoting the
revival of classical learning in England. All his life was
marked by the impulse of withdrawal, the impulse to
detach himself from the worldly environment in which he
was, nevertheless, called on to play such an eminent
role. As a youth he spent four years in a monastery of
the Carthusian order, an order whose members devote
themselves to solitary contemplation in their cells. His
friend Erasmus, who had More's Latin poems printed,
lamented the fact that "England's only genius" had so
little time for literature because of the public demands
on him. He was still in his thirties when, on a diplomatic
mission to the Continent for Henry VIII, he began the

composition of his Utopia, which represents a powerful revulsion against the corrupt existential world in which he was to hold positions of such prominence. Utopia sets forth the contrast between the world as it should be and the world as it is.

More's renown was such, from an early age, that he was under repeated compulsion by the power of the state to participate in public service. He must for years have debated within himself whether it was his duty to accede. This comes out clearly in the passage of Utopia in which he discusses with the world traveler, Raphael Hytholodaye, whether a man of such wide experience as Hytholodaye ought not to enter the service of a king as his advisor. Hytholodaye, who puts his own independence above all other considerations, maintains that in this corrupt world as it is no king would heed the advice of one who spoke as a philosopher for the world as it should be. More agrees, and adds that it would therefore be useless for a king's counselor to advise him in such terms. ("This school philosophy is not unpleasant among friends in familiar communication, but in the counsels of kings, where great matters be debated and reasoned with great authority, these things have no place.") His already considerable experience of practical affairs saves him from Plato's mistake in believing that philosophers can guide the rulers of this world. He goes on to say, however, that, as a king's counselor, "you must with a crafty wile and a subtle design study and endeaver yourself, as much as in you lieth, to handle the matter wisely and suitably for the purpose, and that which you cannot turn to good, so to order it that it be not very bad. For it is not possible for all things to be well, unless all men were good. Which I think will not be yet this good many years."

All those whose bent of mind is contemplative, but who find themselves discharging responsibilities for decision and action, must have the same experience of being two persons at once: on the one hand the person who acts, and on the other the person who shadows the actor as a detached observer. This duality is a distinctive feature of More, as it is of Hamlet. It was with heavy misgivings that he allowed himself to be drawn away from the scholarly life by the King's command: first to undertake diplomatic missions, then to serve as a member of the King's court and the King's Council, finally to become the principal officer of the Crown. He was to have ample occasion to appreciate Socrates's point that, if one would devote oneself to truth and still survive, it can only be in a private station. More devoted himself to truth in a public station, and did not survive. In the end he made the same choice as Socrates in favor of death. And there was the same hesitation, on the part of the King, to take extreme measures against him as there had been on the part of the Athenians to take extreme measures against Socrates—as there was on the part of Marshal Tito to take extreme measures against Milovan Djilas.

The great test came in 1527, when More told the King he could not support his proposal to divorce Catherine of Aragon. This was at the beginning, only, of Henry VIII's career of increasing corruption. (It will be recalled that Henry, succeeding his brother on the throne of England, had also taken his brother's queen as his own.) Henry agreed that More, as a conscientious objector, should be allowed to abstain from participation in anything to do with the divorce, and later that year he appointed him Lord Chancellor, the highest officer of the realm, in succession to Cardinal Wolsey. The King's purpose appears to have been to identify More, to identify his intellectual authority, with a policy of which he did not approve, expecting that he could corrupt him, and More was virtually compelled to accept the office.

During the next five years, however, the King's decision to divorce Catherine and marry Anne Boleyn came to entail a revolt against Rome and the establishment of a separate Catholic Church in England, which would be under Henry and therefore obedient to his bidding in the matter of the divorce. The English ecclesiastical establishment submitted on May 15, 1532, and the next day the author of Utopia resigned as Lord Chancellor.

For two years, then, heavy pressure was put on him to acquiesce in the King's assumption of the head-ship of the Church, the stake being his own life. He stood fast, however, and was finally committed to imprisonment in the Tower of London. His defense, when he was brought to trial, is a classic of the same kind as Socrates's defense in the Apology. On July 1, 1535, he was attainted for treason. Five days later, professing himself "the King's good servant but God's first," he was beheaded on Tower Hill at the age of fifty-seven. He appears to have gone to his death as contentedly as Socrates had gone to his almost two thousand years earlier.

The English churchmen who acquiesced in Henry's seizure of the Church are the counterpart of the courtiers who acquiesced in Claudius's usurpation of the Danish throne—for we may hardly doubt that, among the latter, the fact of the usurpation was not unsuspected. (Hamlet was not alone in his apprehension.) Like Rosen-crantz and Guildenstern, the English churchmen under Henry were governed by the corrupt impulse to serve power, whoever might hold it.

For More truth was, in a sense, simpler than for Socrates or Hamlet. He believed in the fundamental teachings of the one Christian Church that had existed up to his generation, which was also the generation of Luther and Calvin. He was no fanatic or dogmatist, however, but a humanist and church reformer, an advocate of religious tolerance, the close friend and associate of Erasmus, whose life was largely given to purifying a Christianity that had become corrupt. Like Socrates, Erasmus was a believer in "the inner light," and he regarded knowledge as being, with prayer, the way to salvation. When More said he was God's servant first, this was his way of saying that his first allegiance had to be to truth.

6. Shakespeare

All literature is autobiographical in the sense that it represents the author's experience only: his experience of himself in the first place, his experience of others in the second place. For when he describes the thoughts and feelings of others he is describing what he is able to recognize only because he has known it in himself.

I must immediately qualify this to take account of such imitation as plays a major part in all imaginative literature. Being color-blind, I have never seen the color green, but I could give a written account of it with which no one could find fault by repeating in my own words what others have said about it, by imitating their descriptions. If I had never experienced the sexual impulse I could still describe, in a novel, a man's obsessive desire for a woman by adopting, in effect, the accounts of others. This kind of imitation is basic in the great mass of literature, which imitates itself more than it imitates life. Beginning in the 1920's, Ernest Hemingway portrayed fictional characters who spoke in short, abrupt phrases that gave an impression of taciturn virility, but that did not represent the way people speak in reality. This clipped dialogue quickly came to be accepted, however, as representing realism in fiction (by contrast, for example, with the way Henry James's characters talked), and ever since writers who think of themselves as realists have displayed it in their novels. Love and sexual desire, as described in fiction, have also, in all ages, followed fashions that represent literature imitating literature rather than life. In fact, it is life that imitates literature at least as much as literature imitates life. Somerset Maugham once remarked that the Englishmen in Kipling's stories of India were more representative of the generation after he wrote than of that in which he wrote. Young Osric, in Hamlet, is imitating the speech and manners of Lyly's Euphues, a fictional character who had an immense vogue in Shakespeare's day.

Shakespeare, too, has his characters out of stock,

characters more familiar to literature than to life. He also has, like all writers of fiction, characters needed for supporting parts that are not realized in the sense that their inner reality is not represented. Rosencrantz and Guildenstern are such characters, the proof being that they are not differentiated. Undoubtedly Shakespeare knew in himself, as we all do, the impulse to serve power that we assume to be the motive of their acts, but their inner life did not in itself concern him. Fortinbras, too, is not realized. Having an essentially symbolic role, he is seen from outside only. These characters represent the author's experience of life and literature in a large sense, but they have no intimate autobiographical significance.

   With other characters in Shakespeare the situation is ambiguous. I daresay he could not have written Othello as he did if he had not directly experienced the pangs of jealousy; and that he put into Macbeth a remorse that he had himself felt with a terrible poignancy, the same remorse as is expressed in Hamlet's: "I could accuse me of such things that it were better my mother had not borne me." Reading Macbeth and King Henry IV, especially, I have no doubt that Shakespeare knew what it was to suffer from insomnia; and, in fact, a repeated theme of his plays is the inability to sleep associated with high position and responsibility.

   My point is that an author's works may not be significantly autobiographical in detail, but that taken as a whole they are so. One cannot read all the novels of Tolstoy without having an intimate picture of the man in the end—even though one had never been given an inkling of who he was. One would know, for example, that he was a Russian landowner. One would know that he had experienced a certain amount of high-living in his youth and had not abstained from sowing his wild oats. One would know that he, too, had experienced pangs of remorse, and had suffered from an inner moral conflict which at times was almost unendurable.

   Suppose that, having no inkling of who had written

Shakespeare's plays and poems, one asked oneself what they revealed about their author. I am opening here, in this fashion, what has been a question of bitter controversy for some two centuries, and has set off polemics almost uncontrolled in their virulence.

The problem arises for me, as it has for others, because the identity of the author that comes out so vividly in his works does not match the identity of the man to whom they are attributed. The answer that scholarship would make is that the purely subjective impression derived from the works must give way to the attributed identity if the attribution is clearly based on historical evidence. One supposes that the attribution is, indeed, clearly based on such evidence, and the scholars to whom it presents no subjective difficulty see no reason for doubting it. If one assumes, as we all initially do, that the plays and poems were written by a small-town provincial who went to London and became an actor for a number of years before returning to his home, then we are moved to fill out the assumption by making our conclusions on each problem that arises fit it. We persuade ourselves that we know more than we actually do about the actor from Stratford because we know, for example, that he must have been a playwright to have written the plays, we know from the internal evidence of the plays that he was familiar with foreign languages, etc. Consequently, biographical accounts tend to be studded with such qualifying terms as "presumably" and "doubtless," based on the a priori assumption of his authorship. If, however, we omit what is based on this assumption, it is suprising to find that we know almost nothing about this man from Stratford, and that the little we do know is incongruous with his authorship of Shakespeare's works.

The paucity of our basic knowledge, here, has been a prime puzzle even to Shakespeare scholars who do not doubt the man of Stratford's authorship. Professor Schücking, for instance, writes: "The most surprising fact about Shakespeare is not, as is commonly supposed, the contrast between his education and his achievements, but rather that his personality left so slight an impression on the times in which he lived. It is difficult to understand how a playwright, who made a mark on theatrical history that has endured for centuries, . . . should have so little occupied the attention of his contemporaries. . . . [For] great poetical achievements have in all ages brought fame and personal success to their authors. . . . There must therefore be some definite reason why we know so extraordinarily little about Shakespeare—less, indeed, than about any other great genius produced by our western civilization." In default of an alternative plausible to him, Professor Schücking concludes: "The only possible explanation is that he lived in a particularly secluded way, took little part in social life, and came into contact with the public chiefly through his profession as an actor."*

Considering, then, how little real knowledge we have, as distinct from what is presumed, one finds reason to doubt that the attribution is clearly based on historical evidence. One may also find hypothetical explanations, which do not seem far-fetched, for a use of the actor's name to cover an authorship that there was reason to keep secret.

In sum, the picture of the author I derive from the works does not fit the attribution, and when I look into the attribution I find that it is not as solidly based as I had supposed. It does not save me from an agonizing doubt.

Let me turn specifically, now, to the picture of the author that forms in my mind as I read the poems and plays, since it is relevant to the understanding of Hamlet. If I ask myself what is the standpoint from

---

*   Levin L. Schücking, The Meaning of Hamlet, translated from the German by Graham Rawson, London, 1937, pages 9-10.

which these works were written, the answer is that they were written from the standpoint of one who was a member of the higher nobility, or who was so intimately associated with it as to share its point of view altogether. There are no signs, I hasten to add, that the point of view is put on, as by a commoner who, having risen to high place, adopts what is not native to him. All the characters in Shakespeare who are seen intimately from the inside, and who therefore have strong autobiographical implications, are members of the highest aristocracy or, at least, of a ruling group; while all the characters who belong to the common ranks are seen from the outside and are seen, for the most part, from above and at a distance. All the life that is seen intimately from the inside is the life of courts or like centers of power; while the life of the commonality is seen only from above and at a distance. What the author of these plays knows poignantly is what it is to be a great lord, weighed down by the obligations of living up to his station. In no case does he really know what it is to be a commoner down in the ranks. This, I believe, presents a full contrast to the works of such contemporary playrights as Jonson, Marlowe, Webster, and the others.

This picture of the author seems to me self-evident in Hamlet, but not only in Hamlet. I find it as well in King Richard II, in the two parts of King Henry IV, and in King Henry V; I find it in As You Like It; I find it throughout the tragedies, the histories, and the comedies, with a consistency to which I know no exception.

A constant attitude in these plays is that of longing for the simple and uncorrupted life that the common people are thought to lead. One finds this made explicit in As You Like It. One finds it as a repeated theme in the historical plays. One finds it in King Lear. One finds it in The Winter's Tale. One finds something of it in Hamlet's attitude toward those who are outsiders to the court: Horatio, the players, even Rosencrantz and Guildenstern in his initial reception of them. He is not drawn to them as a man is drawn to his own. On the

111

contrary, he is drawn to them as Prince Hal is drawn to the denizens of the Boar's Head Tavern in Eastcheap: they represent escape from the responsibilities that go with high birth, escape from the constrained behavior required at court, escape from ceremonial.

There is no doubt in my own mind that Hamlet is Shakespeare himself. What does it mean, however, to say this ? There must be something of Shakespeare in Othello, too, but this does not mean that Shakespeare was a Moor. Neither was he, to adopt the reductio ad absurdum, the son of the King of Denmark.

In the first instance, we have to distinguish character from topical circumstances. Hamlet is Shakespeare in terms of character. I have no doubt that, just like Hamlet, Shakespeare was introspective; that he was given to musing about life rather than taking action; that he felt a revulsion against the existential world that made the thought of death attractive to him; that he was given to variations of mood from sportive gaiety to profound melancholy; that he found his greatest release from the frustrations of life in words, whether in the poignancy of poetic utterance or in simply unpacking his heart; that he knew self-contempt and such pangs of conscience as made him feel, on occasion, that it were better his mother had not borne him; that he knew both sexual desire and a revulsion from sexual relations (see sonnet CXXIX); and that he found his most abiding refuge from all his inner torments in the philosophical detachment that comes from contemplating the infinite space of the cosmos, the immeasurable magnitude of eternity, the shortness of human life, and the fact that death levels all. Indeed, all these items of character are found more or less prominently in the sonnets, which might have been written by Hamlet as he grew older.

I also have no doubt that Shakespeare was possessed by the normative vision of an ideal world, a world of harmony, order, and gentleness; a hierarchical world in which the upper orders were shepherds ministering to the welfare of the community as a whole; a world in which every man occupied the place assigned him by birth and discharged the duties that went with it; a world in which husbands and wives were constant, in which children were obedient to their fathers and respectful of their mothers; a world in which natural law prevailed, in which transgressors were put down by constituted authority. I also have no doubt that Shakespeare, while outwardly accepting the traditional religious beliefs and forms of his day, was in his inner consciousness the kind of agnostic that Socrates was. The dominance of the normative vision over his mind, his philosophical doubts about it, and the practical necessity he was under of conducting his life in terms of an existential world that, under a complex of pretenses, constantly violated the normative order—all this set up inner strains from which he found relief in the composition of his plays and poems.

If one felt, as one legitimately might, that Hamlet was Shakespeare only within these limits, which represent character rather than circumstances, no problem would arise. I cannot, however, persuade myself that the identification is, in fact, confined to these limits. It is true that the citizen of a small provincial town, who receives at the most a grammar-school education, and who when grown to manhood goes to London where he becomes an actor (if, indeed, the actor is the same as the Stratford man), might plausibly be governed by the inner visions and conflicts found in Hamlet, and that he might seek the resolution of his frustrations by the same devices, including the composition of poetry and drama. The difficulty is that throughout the works of Shakespeare, and especially in Hamlet, the passion of revulsion is specifically directed against conditions that exist in a highly restricted social environment, and there is a constant assumption that these conditions do not exist in other environments. The man who was brought up in Stratford, to which he retired again after a possible spell as an actor in London, might have accumulated passionate resentments against the rural élite such as he had known them in the

113

society of Warwickshire, where his father was a bailiff; he might have accumulated such resentments against the schools of acting referred to so contemptuously in Hamlet's first conversation with Rosencrantz and Guildenstern; but it is hard to believe that he would have felt them in an intimate personal fashion toward the conspiratorial society of the court, and that he would have felt them in terms of a point of view that belongs to a member of that society, which is quite different from the point of view of an outsider who has been slighted or otherwise mistreated by it. It is hard to believe that such a man would be at once so involved, emotionally, in the court society, and so detached from the common society of the realm that he viewed it only with condescension or amusement. What the author of these plays knows intimately and poignantly, as one "to the manner born," is court society; while his knowledge of the common society is distant and naïve.

Surely Hamlet is Shakespeare in more than the elements of his character. There are circumstances other than those I have already mentioned that support the identification. A nobleman by birth, Hamlet is something like a playwright by vocation. Confronted with a frustrating problem, his first move is to write a play about it. He is repeatedly improvising rhymes. He is unhappy in the society of the court, but at his happiest and most relaxed in the company of actors, to whom he still stands, however, in the relation of a high patron.

On the internal evidence of the plays and poems as a whole, and of Hamlet in particular, I should then arrive at the conclusion that they had been written by someone who was so high of birth as to be a member of the royal entourage; a man profoundly maladjusted and in rebellion against the requirements of his birth and station, as Edward VIII was maladjusted and in rebellion; a man who consequently had sought, on occasion, the kind of escape that Prince Hal found in the company of Eastcheap, who found his greatest relief in the composition of the poems and plays, and who consorted with acting companies in connection with the double life

114

he led. (Indeed, in the sonnets Shakespeare is explicit about his high station, his dishonoring of it, and the public disguise under which he maintains his authorship. His station in life is referred to in CXXV, where he identifies himself as one of the lords who carried the canopy over his sovereign in state processions; his failure to live up to it is suggested in a whole series of sonnets of which XXIX, CX, and CXXI are representative; and the fact that he is not writing under his own name is revealed in LXXVI.) Moreover, leading such a double life, he would feel the need to disguise the illicit half of it, perhaps by having one of the actors he associated with lend his name as author of the plays. (So Hamlet might have asked the First Player to present the play-within-the-play as his own composition.) All this would have constituted a semi-innocent conspiracy involving those members of the literary community, including Ben Jonson, who publicly praised "William Shakespeare" as author of the plays.

When, however, one has concluded that the author of the plays must have been a member of the highest nobility at Queen Elizabeth's court one is left with the problem of specific identification. There is one member of the court who fits the picture I have deduced from the plays and poems. Edward de Vere, Earl of Oxford, is Hamlet in his essential character and basic circumstances alike: a lord who by birth stood at the highest level in the realm, who was part of the royal entourage, who was wild and rebellious in his youth, engaging in such escapades as one associates with Prince Hal, who thereby found himself time and again "in disgrace with fortune and men's eyes" (as Shakespeare reported himself in Sonnet XXIX); a man who, moreover, was considered one of the first poets of the realm until he suddenly stopped issuing poetry under his own name, which was before the first works of "William Shakespeare" were issued; a man who, according to a contemporary chronicler, Francis Meres, was one of "the best for comedy amongst us"; a man who throughout his life had a passion for plays and devoted himself to the patronage of actors, with whom he was closely associated.

115

Is there some other explanation of what is surely a great mystery ?

Perhaps there is. A body of literature has accumulated on the subject, and investigations go on. For my own part, I have to leave the matter at this point. I cannot believe that the man of Stratford wrote the plays, and I am strongly disposed to believe that de Vere was the actual author.

What I am presenting in these pages is simply a personal view of what Hamlet means. I must let that view speak for itself, carrying only such conviction as it may have intrinsically in a straightforward presentation.

It seems to me that in an essential sense, although not literally, the play is for Shakespeare, himself, the equivalent of what the defense offered by Socrates in the Apology was for Socrates. Having been "in disgrace with fortune and men's eyes," he was like Hamlet concerned with his own posthumous vindication. To Horatio Hamlet says, at the last: "O God ! Horatio, what a wounded name, things standing thus unknown, shall live behind me." He asks Horatio to do for him what Plato did for Socrates.

Hamlet's lonely opposition to his environment—to the common mind that dominates it, to the fashions in thought that sway it, to its corruption—establishes a basis of elemental identification with Socrates, Sir Thomas More, Voltaire, and Milovan Djilas. Beyond that, any of us who feel a bond of sympathetic understanding with him are able to feel it only because we have at least a touch of him in ourselves. Surely, however, the historical figure who is Hamlet above all others is Shakespeare himself, whoever he may have been. If, then, we think of the play as being essentially autobiographical, its meaning becomes at once richer and more plausible.

Just as Hamlet is only nominally a Dane and really an Elizabethan lord, so the Danish court of the play, in its essential character, is the Tudor court as the author of _Hamlet_ knew it. The characters in the play were taken, in some cases more literally and in others less, from life. One has the impression that in Osric, for example, Shakespeare had in mind not only a type of courtier that he found both irritating and contemptible, but a specific person. (In _King Henry IV_, Part One, I,3, is it not essentially the same little lord whom Hotspur is referring to when he speaks about the courtier who came out on the battlefield at Holmedon to demand his prisoners on the King's behalf ?) Otherwise, why does he bring in the fact, irrelevant to the play itself, that he had great land-holdings. When Horatio says he does not know Osric, Hamlet replies:

> Thy state is the more gracious; for 'tis
> a vice to know him. He hath much land, and
> fertile: let a beast be lord of beasts, and
> his crib shall stand at the king's mess: 'tis
> a chough; but, as I say, spacious in the
> possession of dirt.

Shakespeare, in what Hamlet says about Osric (here and just after his exit), is surely finding release for a specific personal irritation. Sir Thoms More must have felt the same way about some of the "choughs" at the court of Elizabeth's father.

It is, above all, hard to doubt, and in fact it is generally recognized, that Polonius is Lord Burghley. Elizabeth's principal minister, until his death at the age of seventy-eight, had at the time _Hamlet_ was written become an old busybody who should have been super-annuated long before. His daughter it was whom Oxford married, as Hamlet should have married Polonius's daughter.

I make no argument, however, on the basis of speculative parallels like this. It is the general scene of the court, its fashions and its intrigues, that Shakespeare is describing from the position of an insider like Hamlet, who has been the victim of its hostility toward those who do not play the game. What he is describing in the largest sense is the irremediable corruption of the post-expulsion world that manifests itself most intensely at the centers of power, becoming more bland as one moves out from them—through the academic world represented by Wittenberg to the rustic societies of the simple country folk—until, as he believed, innocence and "infinite heart's ease" is at last found in the hovel of:

> the wretched slave,
> Who with a body filled and vacant mind
> Gets him to rest, crammed with distressful bread;
> Never sees horrid night, the child of hell,
> But, like a lackey, from the rise to set
> Sweats in the eye of Phoebus, and all night
> Sleeps in Elysium; next day after dawn,
> Doth rise and help Hyperion to his horse,
> And follows so the ever-running year
> With profitable labour to his grave.

7. Random Observations

As with all great literature, there are in Hamlet different levels of specificity or abstraction at which interpretation can be pitched. For example, in the bedroom scene when Hamlet lectures his mother, what he is doing is to draw for her the contrast between his father and his uncle. However, at another level, which represents the truth of the play no less, he is drawing the contrast between two worlds: the normative and the existential. Again: in his concern with the impropriety represented by his mother's marriage to the man who is her brother by an earlier marriage—a state of affairs that at least borders on incest—he is concerned with the betrayal of the normative world. The same point can be made with the question whether Hamlet's animus is based on his uncle's murder of his father, or his pollution of his mother, or his defeat of his own ambition to become king.

May we not say that the greatness of all great literature, art, and music is in its expanding reverberations; that its greatness is in the general implications of the particulars with which it deals, in the tendency of its literal meanings to undergo enlargement until they constitute a vision of the whole world ? It seems to me that one could follow the meaning of Hamlet outward until one had included all metaphysics, all ethics, and all political philosophy as well.

Ernest Jones, as a disciple of Freud, found a meaning of the play in Hamlet's libido and his consequent attitudes (subconscious) toward his mother, toward his father, toward Ophelia. Such a meaning would not necessarily be inconsistent with other meanings, or with the large philosophical meaning that constitutes a vision of the world. We should not think in terms of mutually exclusive alternatives.

+   +   +

I know of no other major writer who is so impressed as Shakespeare was by the role that lust may play behind a woman's façade of innocence or respectability. In Venus and Adonis it is Venus, moved by lust, who tries to seduce a young boy. The eponymous heroine of Troilus and Cressida (supposed to have been written at the same period as Hamlet) is entirely governed by sexual desires which lead her into promiscuity. This is the weakness of Queen Gertrude, and Hamlet sees it as at least potential in Ophelia. Therefore it may not be irrelevant to note that Oxford, having married Lord Burghley's daughter in 1571, separated himself from her in 1576, accusing her of having committed adultery during his absence on the Continent. This accusation, however, may well have been only the product of his jealous imaginings, for he later took her back as his wife. Shakespeare's awareness of the injustices that may be produced by an obsessive jealousy is expressed in Othello, in Cymbeline, and in The Winter's Tale with a poignancy so intense as to suggest self-horror.

+ + +

The clue to the main difficulties of human society, and of Hamlet's difficulties in particular, is in the Eleventh Chapter of <u>Genesis</u>. "Now the whole earth had one language and few words." This enabled men to work together and, working together, to build a civilization. However, when this happened the Lord came down to see what the sons of men had built, and he said: "'Behold, they are one people, and they have all one language; and this is only the beginning of what they will do; and nothing that they propose to do will now be impossible for them.'" And in a terrible moment he said: "'Come, let us go down, and there confuse their language, that they may not understand one another's speech.' So the Lord scattered them abroad from there over the face of all the earth, and they left off building the city." This was like a second expulsion.

Shakespeare, one surmises, had the experience of all men who do not represent the common mind. The Poloniuses, the Osrics, and the rest (even the Horatios) did not understand him when he tried to speak of what was deep in him. It was the consequent frustration that impelled him to write <u>Hamlet</u>.

A simile may represent the problem that the Lord created for us all at the site of an unfinished city. About one man in two hundred, having the commonest form of color-blindness, never has seen the color green and never will. This involves minor frustrations for him on occasion, but it poses no serious problem. Suppose, however, that the ratio were reversed, that one person in two hundred could see the color green, while the other 199 could not. When this one person spoke of a color not generally recognized or named, describing it and commenting on it, the generality of mankind would not know what he was talking about. If he persisted they would begin to think he was mentally disordered, and in any case he would find that he aroused the hostility with which the common mind instinctively responds to individual vision. Such a person would have to learn, then, to live his life with a major problem that he could never resolve.

There can be no doubt that each of us, looking at the same scene, sees something different, since each of us has different eyes, a different mind, different conditioning by training and experience. (No two of us read the same play when we read Hamlet.) A common mind—without which we should find ourselves in anarchy, unable to work together or survive at all—is possible because the differences are for the most part minor. An exceptional individual may, however, have a vision of the world that, as he discovers with experience, no one else sees, even though it is so vivid for him that he cannot understand how others could fail to see it. He then finds himself with the same problem as that of the prodigy who can see green, but more serious in his case because what is involved is so much more significant than one color in the visible spectrum.

Matters of degree are involved here. In my simile, the man who can see green will find one other person in two hundred who can see it. (Of those who were physically able to see it, however, perhaps forty-nine out of fifty would, nevertheless, not see it, simply because the society in which they lived did not see it, so that in fact he would find far fewer than one in two hundred.) Socrates was not understood by the common mind of Athens, which reacted with the hostility repre-sented by Aristophanes (as well as Anytus and Meletus), but he did have followers like Plato who, in greater or lesser degree, were able to apprehend his meaning. And Thomas More had Erasmus.

I have now described Hamlet's basic plight, which was certainly Shakespeare's. The author of the plays and poems had a vision of the world that moved him profoundly. Initially, he assumed that others saw it too. When he spoke in terms of it, however, he found that he was not understood at all. He also found that he often could not understand the terms in which those who represented the common mind spoke, terms which everyone else understood. We may suppose that these mutual failures of understanding involved him in difficulties from the earliest days of his childhood associations with other children. The gulf between him and them provoked them to combine against him. He was made to feel deficient, and he was made to doubt whether his own vision was valid. Still, to the extent that his vision was vivid, and to the extent that it seemed to him a revelation of the nature of the world, he was irresistably moved to express it—like another Ancient Mariner. Although he had been trained to the common mind, and strove to make it his own, the difference of his own mind was bound to show itself at every turn.

Such a man, given to introspection and sometimes in a torment of frustration, would constantly seek to escape from the constricting circle in which his life was cast. Like Hamlet, he might seek the company of actors and playwrights. Stimulated by the association, he would try his own hand at composition, initially adopting the standard forms and conventions (as Shakespeare did in **Venus and Adonis**.) He might write dramas of murder and intrigue, initially in an imitative spirit. The dramas would, however, become vehicles for the vision that he could not help expressing, that came out in spite of himself. It would, perhaps, tend to dominate what had been basically, say, simply a drama about murder and intrigue at a legendary Danish court. There would, then, be those who enjoyed the drama for its blood and thunder alone; but there would be others who were aware, even if only dimly, of some larger world implicitly revealed, so that they came away from its performance with a feeling of having themselves been enlarged— enlarged not just in the sense of having had their own understanding broadened, but also in the sense of having been liberated from the narrowness of the corrupt existential environment. The works of Shakespeare would be appreciated for different qualities by different persons according to their aptitudes. Because those works did, however, have something that enlarged people, even though it was difficult to identify or define, they would continue to be performed and read for century after century. So, when the local scene to which Shakespeare had stood opposed had long passed away, and when all the passion associated with that scene had long been spent, he would in the survival of his work, which was himself, prove to have been justified. This is a major theme of the sonnets, the only works in which he spoke directly for himself in the first person.

+   +   +

The King, the Queen, Polonius, Fortinbras—all the characters in Hamlet except one—live exclusively in the here-and-now. They are totally preoccupied with whatever is the problem of the moment. One cannot, for example, imagine Fortinbras wondering whether there was any point to conquering the land he coveted in Poland since, after all, it wouldn't make any difference in two hundred years.

What distinguishes man from the beasts, however, is the capacity for a vision of the world that transcends the immediate. The most primitive tribes known, closest to the beasts in this, have not been aware of the connection between sexual intercourse and the phenomenon of birth, too long delayed for them to make the connection in their minds. The most educated men of today, however, live in a universe that extends back many billions of years, and that extends outward to such a distance that a beam of light, traveling at 186,000 miles per second, requires ten billion years to traverse it. Contrast this with the world of the earthworm.

The difference between Hamlet and his fellow men is that he lives in a larger world. He has wide-angle vision. In this, too, he is Shakespeare—and Shakespeare would surely have understood the remark of the Chinese philosopher, Chuang-tzu, that it is no use speaking to the frog in the well of the great ocean.

+   +   +

Throughout the plays Shakespeare's nobility or elevation of thought is cast into verse, prose being reserved for what is mundane, commonplace, or low in other respects. The prose speeches of Hamlet constitute an exception. They have, repeatedly, a largeness of view and a depth of feeling not matched in most of the verse he utters. I am close to saying that I prefer his prose to his verse.

The explanation must be that, being fundamentally a man of reason, he expresses himself best in the language of reason. The best passages in French literature are prose, the French language being better suited to prose than to verse precisely because the French mind too, at its best, is a reasoning mind. I have referred to Hamlet's vision, but it is not the romantic vision of a Byron. It is more like the rational vision of a Bacon, a Hobbes, or a Newton. Hamlet is primarily a man of intellect (there is much of the eighteenth-century Enlightenment in him), and this makes prose his natural medium.

+   +   +

It is a truism that Shakespeare loved the language, that he found a release from his frustration in the designs and formulations he fashioned out of it. This is what all who are writers by vocation do. Hamlet was quite aware of the fact that he was, himself, doing it, that it was his alternative to action. But he was not at his best with the language when this was all he was doing.

The most extreme example of this escape into language is found in Richard II. Simply in terms of talent, he is the most gifted literary figure in Shakespeare. Confronted with a requirement for action that he cannot meet, since he is no more a man of action than

Hamlet, he finds his outlet in poetical utterance more beautiful, in its way, than anything else in the plays:

> For God's sake, let us sit upon the ground
> And tell sad stories of the death of kings.

He retreats from the problems of the existential world into delusions that are pitiful or absurd, but graced with the grace of language:

> Not all the water in the rough rude sea
> Can wash the balm from an anointed king.

He could not say such a thing in prose because prose is taken more literally than verse, which makes what it says more vulnerable to criticism. (I have never shared the view that poetry is the more disciplined language. On the contrary, for many modern poets at least, it provides an escape from the discipline of language which is the discipline of thought. By being delphic, as poetry allows one to be, one makes oneself immune to criticism— even to self-criticism where one is privately unsure of one's own meaning.)

Richard is a weak and pitiful character, but with an incomparable gift for language. With intellectual and moral strength added, he might have been another Hamlet. He, too, should not have been born a prince.

+   +   +

Shakespeare, as the sonnets show, foresaw his own immortality; but surely he did not foresee centuries of a Shakespearian scholarship so thorough that it would subject every word considered his to exhaustive analysis and exegesis. Such foreknowledge might have frightened him into silence. As it is, there are inconsistencies in Hamlet that I think are best explained simply by the fact that he was human.

One is that Polonius, who otherwise utters nothing that does not show him to be a fool, sends Laertes off to

France with a string of precepts that represent perfect wisdom of their kind. For a moment he is as wordly wise as Prospero, as shrewd as Portia. I was tempted, in my running commentary, to explain this as an indication that he had been a man of wisdom before he fell into his dotage—but I caught myself in time.

Another inconsistency is that Hamlet is a university student, presumably still in his 'teens, until he returns from his broken voyage to England. Then, in the grave-diggers' scene, it transpires that he is thirty years old. Since he has matured conspicuously since we last saw him, one is tempted to justify this as poetic truth. However, I was able to master this temptation too.

Horatio sometimes is represented as a complete outsider to the court, a poor student who comes on a visit from Wittenberg. At other times he is represented as a born member of the Court who speaks with its authority. When we ask which he really was we should recall that as a fictional character he never actually lived, so that the question of his reality is inapposite.

Hamlet's doubt of any life after death, as he expresses it in his third soliloquy, is inconsistent with the credence he gives his father's ghost. However, I take the ghost to be a theatrical device only, repre-senting Hamlet's inner consciousness. Even without this explanation, however, the inconsistency would be plausible in terms of the common habit, among us limited and bedeviled men, of dividing our minds into two compartments, in one of which each of us is a believer and does not question, in the other of which he is a questioner and does not believe.

8.   The Meaning of Meaning

Literature belongs with music, painting, and sculpture as one of the imaginative arts. There have been great ages when these arts, in one or another of their branches, flourished, and there have been others when one can only say that, even though they continued to be practiced, they were dead. "All the noblest arts," Samuel Butler wrote, "hold in perfection but a very little moment. They soon reach a height from which they begin to decline, and when they have begun to decline it is a pity that they cannot be knocked on the head." In the ages when they are really dead, although still practiced, their practice represents the pretence that has been one theme of this discussion. It represents the existential world submerged, at last, in its own corruption.

I see some evidence of this in our own time. At least in music, in poetry, in painting, and in sculpture, there has been a primary preoccupation with forms and techniques. Composers have felt that the diatonic scale and the traditional harmonies were too restrictive; poets have felt that the old regularities of meter were too restrictive; painters and sculptors have felt that the confinement of their arts to representation was too restrictive. Consequently, for the best part of a century now there has been a highly self-conscious rebellion against these forms which has manifested itself in experiments that dispense with them. There has also been experimentation in new techniques, like those of electronic music, mobile sculpture, and invented vocabularies—all designed, it is said, to break the confinement of traditional forms and techniques within which artistic expression has hitherto been held.

What, however, do we mean by artistic expression ? When we say that a form is too restrictive for what the artist wants to express we imply that what he wants to express is too large for the form—too large for a sonnet or a sonata, too large for conventional instruments of music or conventional syntax.

One is brought to ask, then, what it is that the artist wants to express in terms of his legitimate function. We agree, after all, that art is communication, and communication is the communication of—what ?

The question is not easily answered without begging it. Throughout the nineteenth century most poets, at least in the English language, would have said that their mission was to communicate something called "beauty." This points a direction (which the poets of our own day have abjured) but does not get us very far. We take an essential step forward, I think, when we consult Keats and are told that "beauty is truth." But this, too, needs interpreting (which I have elsewhere had the temerity to undertake at length: e.g., my Men and Nations).

Most serious novelists would say that their mission is to put the reality of life, in one or another of its manifestations, on paper. Well, I should hope so ! But, will any manifestation of reality do as well as any other ? A good deal of our daily life is, surely, too dull to be memorialized. Listen, however, to Joseph Conrad on his function as a novelist:

> The ethical view of the universe involves us at last in so many cruel and absurd contradictions, where the last vestiges of faith, hope, charity, and even of reason itself, seem ready to perish, that I have come to suspect that the aim of creation cannot be ethical at all. I would fondly believe that its object is purely spectacular: a spectacle for awe, love, adoration, or hate, if you like, but in this view—and in this view alone— never for despair ! Those visions, delicious or poignant, are a moral end in themselves. The rest is our affair—the laughter, the tears, the tenderness, the indignation, the high tranquility of a steeled heart, the detached curiousity of a subtle mind—that's our affair ! And the unwearied self-forgetful attention to every phase of the living universe reflected in our consciousness may be our appointed task on this earth. A task in which fate has perhaps engaged nothing of us except our conscience, gifted with a voice in order to bear true testimony to the

visible wonder, the haunting terror, the infinite passion and the illimitable serenity; to the supreme law and the abiding mystery of the sublime spectacle.

Elsewhere, Conrad remarks that he has "never sought in the written word anything else but a form of the Beautiful."

At this point, I think, a satisfactory answer to our question confronts us at last. Conrad, like most serious modern novelists (I omit the Harriet Beecher Stowes, who have another justification), disavows any ethical purpose and claims only to represent reality as "a spectacle." As soon as he begins to identify the spectacle, however, a personal or subjective element comes in quite overwhelmingly. Conrad, it is evident, has a personal vision that he identifies with the reality of the spectacle—for it is not in itself or in the eyes of just anyone that it represents "the visible wonder, the haunting terror, the infinite passion and the illimitable serenity. . . the supreme law and the abiding mystery. . . ." We need Conrad in order to see it that way ourselves.

Here, I think, we have our answer. What the artist has to express, what he has to communicate, is a personal vision. He is moved by the natural impulse we all have, from first childhood, when we see something that impresses us, to take others by the sleeve and say, "Look what I see !" This applies equally to the various branches of literature, to music, to painting, to sculpture—all of which are simply different media for expressing personal vision.

If somebody tells me, then, that music should no longer be limited by the diatonic scale, or painting by representation, I am willing to agree. Bravo ! But first I want to know what it is, specifically, that the old forms are holding back. Implicit in the proposition is some personal vision that cannot be got within them, and their inadequacy is such in relation to that vision. After

129

all, there is nothing restrictive about hobbling a horse that is dead.

The question arises when one has to witness what use most experimental artists make of their freedom from traditional forms. This is so disappointing, to me personally, as to lead me to the mournful conclusion that, having no personal vision at all to preoccupy them, they are experimenting with forms and techniques for their own sake. Worse than this, I think they are playing the same fashionable game as the young intellectuals who, in the lobbies of concert-halls, in the art galleries, or at literary cocktail-parties chatter over the works that these artists present for the purposes of the game.

I come back to what seems to me fundamental. Earlier in these remarks I said that, while the man of action saves the present, it is the contemplative individual who saves the future, allowing us to hope that we may some day emerge from the tragic dilemmas of this post-paradisial age. He does so by enlarging the common understanding of mankind, and he enlarges the common understanding by the personal vision that he communicates through works of philosophy, of science, or of imaginative art in the generic sense of the term.

We all of us have our conceptions of the world, which we may call visions, but in most cases they represent the parochial vision of the common mind, as it exists at a particular time and place, in a particular group. There are those, too, who have essentially insane visions of their own, like the little fanatic who warns us that the world will end on Friday. Then there are those who have a nihilistic view, a sort of anti-vision: the world, they announce, has no meaning. These people are not necessarily fraudulent, consciously or even unconsciously, but they make no contribution to the enlargement of understanding.

The individuals who contribute to the enlargement of understanding are few, they are bound to lead lonely and frustrating lives, and often they end badly—at least from a wordly point of view. Shakespeare was one of these few, and <u>Hamlet</u> is remarkable, I think, because in it he gave us, as nowhere else, what is essentially his own portrait. In thus giving us a portrait of genius, he invested us with the vision of a universe dominated by the tragic conflict of two irreconcilable worlds.

———————————

NOTE ON SOURCES AND CITATIONS

I have used W.J. Craig's Oxford text in the citations, allowing myself, however, to make such minor changes as "promised" for "promis'd" (where it is evident in either case that the syllable is silent); and twice, where I have preferred the rendering of the Cambridge New Shakespeare, edited by J. Dover Wilson, I have used that instead. I have also, on occasion, quoted the stage-directions as given in the latter. Finally, a small matter: I have referred to "grave-diggers" rather than "clowns" because they are not clowns in the modern sense. Both have something of Hamlet in them.

I have quoted the Jowett translation of Plato as rendered by Sir R.W. Livingstone in his presentation of it under the title, Portrait of Socrates, Oxford, 1938.

I have used Raphe Robynson's English translation of 1551 from the original Latin of More's Utopia, as presented with the original punctuation and orthography under the editorship of J. Rawson Lumby, Cambridge, 1879; but in quoting from it I have made my own modernization of language and spelling. An account of More's defense at his trial may be found in R.W. Chambers, Thomas More, London, 1935, V, II.

The two quotations of Joseph Conrad are, respectively, from A Personal Record, New York, 1934, pp. 92 and xxi.

ODYSSEUS AND THE FUTURE

Note: A much abridged version of this essay appears as Part Five, Chapter IV of my <u>Out of Chaos</u>, Boston, 1977.

What accounts for the sense of absolute satisfaction, of fulfillment, with which one finishes The Odyssey ?

The happy ending might explain it. After ten years of agonizing frustration, through which the reader suffers with him, Odysseus wins his way back, at last, to his wife, his son, and his kingdom, to which he restores the order that had broken down in his absence.

We have all experienced a thousand times the satisfaction that happy endings provide—in the fairy-tales of our childhood, in light fiction, in the movies, even in the cartoon-strips of newspapers. This is the satisfaction we feel when we come to the end of The Odyssey. By a delicious anticipation, moreover, we taste it throughout the long tale of the hero's sufferings and frustrations—for, as in the case of Hamlet, no one reads The Odyssey without knowing in advance how it is going to end. Our pleasurable anticipation becomes more intense as, chapter-by-chapter, Odysseus approaches the day when he will land on the shores of Ithaca, overthrow the usurping suitors, and be reunited with his wife and son. At last, when all that we knew would happen does happen, we feel ourselves more than fulfilled, exalted.

As far as it goes, this seems to me a valid explanation of the satisfaction one feels at the end of The Odyssey. But there must be more to it than that, unless we accept T.E. Lawrence's judgment that The Odyssey is merely light entertainment composed by the world's first novelist. If our satisfaction is deeper and more abiding than what we derive from just any tale with a happy ending, then the explanation, however valid in itself, is not enough.

The happy ending of The Odyssey is associated

with a normative vision, and this, surely, is what lifts it to a higher plane of literature. All of us, living as we must in a world of disorder, strive for the realization of a normative order that we cherish in our minds, a conception of what God or nature intended us to be, a conception of how God or nature intended us to live. All of us, consequently, inhabit two worlds at once: the existential world of accident, conflict, sordidness, and breakdown, the world of greed and hatred, of cowardice and treachery—this on the one hand, and on the other a world of the imagination in which a Pythagorean harmony prevails, in which all men fulfill the roles reserved for them in the sublime pageant of life as it was intended to be, as we have sometimes thought it must have been before men fell into evil, as we hope it will be at the end of all our striving.

Each of us has in his mind a conception of propriety that contrasts with the world of his actual experience, even though we disagree in our respective conceptions (as our ideological conflicts show). For some, such propriety is represented by the vision of St. Paul; for others, by that of Karl Marx. Some have found it in Hitler's **Mein Kampf**, others in **The Little Flowers of St. Francis of Assisi**. Some have found it in the ideal Confucian order, in which men are organized about the family unit, others in the ideal order of Maoism, in which they are organized in the equivalent of barracks.

The normative order of the Homeric vision is one that has, so far, prevailed in a wide variety of disparate societies separated from one another in time or space. It is a hierarchical order within which men and women have each their obligations of leadership or obedience according to their place in the whole. As has generally been true of agricultural societies, the fundamental unit is the family, based on the lifelong mutual attachment of husband and wife. The organized societies of the Homeric world were small and local, exemplified by Pylos and Sparta, by Ithaca, by Troy and Mycenae. In each the husband and father who was the head of the leading family was also king. He was responsible for the leadership and protection of the community, while the others had the duty of obedience according to their respective stations, whether as sons, as soldiers, as artisans, as thralls, as wives, or as handmaidens. The kings, themselves, might be loosely leagued together, with bonds of mutual obligation not unlike those among the lords of our own feudal age, two thousand years after Homer's day. The expedition to Troy under Agamemnon's leadership represented the discharge by him and the other kings of a collective obligation to uphold the union between Menelaus and his wife Helen. Each had once been Helen's suitor; in their mutual rivalry Menelaus had won her; all had accepted the legitimacy of the victory so won; and all had agreed to uphold the normative order as represented by the relationship between husband and wife so established.

What The Iliad recounts is a catastrophic disruption of this normative order in consequence of pettiness on the part of gods and men alike. Aphrodite had engendered the catastrophe by promising Paris the enjoyment of an illegitimate union with Helen if he would award her, rather than Hera or Athena, the golden apple of victory as the most beautiful of the godesses. In payment of that bribe she had enabled him to steal Helen from Menelaus and carry her off to Troy. This was the act that, by disrupting the normative order, would have such terrible and far-reaching consequences.

Odysseus, still in full enjoyment of that order as the king in far-away Ithaca—with his young wife, Penelope, and his new-born son, Telemachus—foreboded these consequences, and tried to evade his obligation of involvement like many draft-evaders since (by feigning insanity), but without success. He, too, had to abandon his normal life and go to Troy.

The Iliad is a partial account of the existential chaos represented by the ten-years' siege of Troy, ending in sordid death and destruction for Greeks and Trojans alike. What Priam, the Trojan king, and his

137

family have to suffer is too horrible to contemplate. But to the leader of the Greeks, Agamemnon, comes a doom on the same scale. Returning to his home after ten years, he is taken in ambush and murdered by his wife and her lover, who thereby set off a new succession of sordid disasters that will afflict his line for generations to come. All this in consequence of the disruption of the normative order by the dirty little deal between Aphrodite and Paris.

A like disorder threatens finally to engulf the house and line of Odysseus in Ithaca. With the throne empty, and the place of Penelope's husband vacant in her bed, a lawless crew of upstarts from Ithaca and the surrounding islands make themselves at home in Odysseus' palace, spurn his son, and lay siege to the unhappy Penelope. This is the situation that is revealed to the reader at the beginning of The Odyssey, and we then follow Odysseus as, against heartbreaking obstacles and setbacks, he strives for ten years to win his way back to his home, where in the end he will redeem a wife who has been faithful as the wives of Menelaus and Agamemnon were not, where he will kill the usurpers and restore the normative order that had been disrupted when Paris carried off Helen. This, and not some merely personal triumph, is the happy ending.

+   +   +

Every work of literature is the varying product of what the author wrote and what each reader reads. To the extent that the reader represents the times in which he lives, then, the work changes with the changing times. T.E. Lawrence belonged to a time that, in reaction to the Victorian Age's affectation of lofty sentiment, affected the deflation of pretentiousness. When, at the beginning of the 1930s, he wrote the introduction to his translation of The Odyssey, he did so in the prevalent mood of "debunking." "Obviously the tale was the thing," he wrote; and, "the author misses his every chance of greatness, as must all his faithful translators." Odysseus is "that cold-blooded egotist,"

Telemachus "the priggish son."

I speculate that, in any case, the normative vision could not have had much meaning for Lawrence. He never married, never acquired a family, never had a home to return to, was less attached to his native country than to foreign lands. When the adventurous period of his life was over, with no other place to go he joined the Royal Air Force, attempting to divest himself of his identity in a barracks life, to find a living equivalent of death while awaiting the merciful arrival of that end in its actuality. Although he had lived a life of Odyssean adventure, then, he had lived it without the steadfast purpose of Odysseus. There was never any Penelope he longed to see. There was never any Telemachus, never a rugged shore of Ithaca toward which the lost wanderer ceaselessly sought to make his way. Claiming to deduce the character of Homer "from his self-betrayal in the work," Lawrence concluded that he was driven to legend, "where he found men living untrammelled under the God-possessed sky." But Homer, expressing himself through the character of his hero, was as far as he could be from regarding this nomadic life, "untrammelled under the God-possessed sky," as a blessing. The conception of it as an ideal, rather than as the opposite of an ideal, belongs to Lawrence himself. It fits the picture of the homeless one, escaping from an England in which he could find no abiding place, to live the life of nomadic Arab warriors in their tents under distant skies, untrammelled by any female presence. No wonder he can describe Penelope as "the sly cattish wife" ! But this is not Homer's conception.

To Lawrence, the adventurous all-male life at a distance from one's native country was lived for its own sake, and so he was uncomprehending of the purpose and the vision that drove Odysseus for ten years to get past that life, in spite of every obstacle posed by gods or men, in order to return to a "normal" life. It was because the normative vision of Homer did not exist for Lawrence that he could see in The Odyssey nothing more than a tale of adventure under the God-possessed sky.*

Robert Graves, writing his compilation of Greek Myths in the 1950s, was most alert for whatever bore on the sexual pecadilloes of the mortals and immortals who people the myths, and especially on any aberrations. He writes like a gossip at last freed from traditional taboos, and goes into scandals that we hadn't been told about before. There is even some sniggering, as when he cannot quite bring himself to believe that Penelope really remained chaste during her husband's long absence—although, he admits, "the Odyssey nowhere directly suggests that Penelope has been unfaithful" to him. (On the contrary, her faithfulness is half the theme of the poem.) There is a question, he hints, whether she did not have an affair with Amphinomus of Dulichium, even whether the bed of Odysseus was not familiar to "all the suitors" ! This is sheer nihilism, representing the maliciously destructive impulse.

Yet The Odyssey endures, age after age, because it does have a larger meaning than either Lawrence or Graves found in it.

+   +   +

Sexual fidelity in The Odyssey is governed by a double standard at odds with the normative thinking of

---

*   Mrs. G. Bernard Shaw, old enough to be Lawrence's mother, actually stood in the intimate relationship of a mother-confessor. In 1929 he wrote her: "As for feeling at home with you: that is not the word. I do not wish to feel at home. . . . Homes are ties, and with you I am quite free, somehow." (Quoted by Colin Simpson and Phillip Knightley in the Sunday Times Weekly Review, London, 30 June 1968.) This was the disposition, personal to himself, that he attributed to Odysseus in flat opposition to the evidence of the latter's ten-year struggle to get home.

our own time. As in virtually all societies that in the past have upheld the institution of monogamous marriage, the husband is allowed more latitude than the wife. The Odyssey, while it is clear on Penelope's successful resistance to the suitors, does not suggest that Odysseus had any compunctions about accepting Circe's invitation to share her bed during the year that he lived with her. Yet this in no way diminishes the reader's impression of his unwavering devotion to Penelope, his loyalty to their lifelong marriage. One feels that, in what is essential, he remains as faithful to her as she to him. He also lived with Calypso, her prisoner for seven years on the island of Ogygia, and she offered him immortality if he would consent to remain forever as her husband, but he was not tempted. His single-minded purpose to return to the normative order, of which his marriage was an essential part, never weakened. And the marriage, itself, is no less solid for these evanescent affairs when at last the partners have been reunited.

If this double standard is to be justified at all, it is by the common observation that men can, more easily than women, enter into passing affairs that leave them emotionally unmarked. (Moreover, when progeny ensue, infidelity by women, unlike infidelity by men, may put in question the identity of the biological father.)

+   +   +

If The Odyssey is not just a tale of adventure, as Lawrence would have it, neither is it one of those modern novels that has for its purpose the description of our daily life. What it describes, rather, is life lifted to the level of a heroic ideal. There is one crucial incident, however, that would be worthy of the most sophisticated psychological novelists of our time.

All through the twenty years of their separation Odysseus and Penelope had hoped against hope, and had constantly longed for the day of his homecoming; but to neither had it occurred that, if the day came at last, it might entail embarrassment or disappointment. One has only to consider the situation, however, to see that it was bound to entail an awkward pause, at least, when the two met. After twenty years neither could be, still, the same person the other had known, which means that they would meet as strangers. This would put it in doubt whether the mutual knowledge and understanding that constituted the real marriage-bond still existed. The resumption of intimacy could not be taken for granted.

Penelope is in her upper chamber, quite unaware of the fact that the old beggar who has entered the halls is Odysseus in disguise, unaware of the fact that behind locked doors he has just encompassed the death of the suitors. Now the old nurse, laughing hysterically, comes to break the news to her. Uncertain, hesitating, half alarmed, she agrees to follow the old woman down to the hall, but says disengenuously, "I will go to see my son," adding, "so that I can see my suitors lying dead— and the man who killed them."

> She spoke, and came down from the chamber, her heart pondering much, whether to keep away and question her dear husband, or to go up to him and kiss his head, taking his hands. But then, when she came in and stepped over the stone threshold, she sat across from him in the firelight, facing Odysseus, by the opposite wall . . . .*

Odysseus, too, is reserved now. Twenty years have passed, and he, too, cannot know whether this woman is still his wife. He sits at the other side of the hall looking down at the ground. It is an awful moment, wholly unexpected, and upsetting to the unseasoned Telemachus.

---

* The quotations of Homer are reproduced with per-mission from Richmond Lattimores' The Odyssey of Homer: A Modern Translation, copyright 1965, 1967 by R. Lattimore. I have, however, given them the format of prose rather than set them in the broken lines of the original.

He upbraids his mother, saying that "no other woman
. . . would keep back as you are doing from her
husband who, after much suffering, came at last in the
twentieth year back to his own country."

> My child [says Penelope], the spirit that is
> in me is full of wonderment, and I cannot
> find anything to say to him, nor question
> him, nor look him straight in the face. But
> if he is truly Odysseus, and he has come
> home, then we shall find other ways, and
> better, to recognize each other, for we have
> signs that we know of between the two of us
> only, but they are secret from others.

Because Telemachus is in the way, his father asks him
to leave.

When he is at last alone with Penelope, except for
the presence of the old nurse, Odysseus begins: "You
are so strange. . . ." He blames her, as Telemachus
had, for keeping back from her husband "who, after
much suffering, came at last in the twentieth year back
to his own country."

Penelope, answering, also begins with "You are so
strange. . . ." Both are looking for the key that will
unlock their old identities and thereby restore their
union. Odysseus finds it, at last, by describing
peculiarities of their marriage bed that only he among
men can know. Immediately a common memory restores
the past to the living, the living to the past. Penelope's
"knees and her heart went slack." Then "she burst into
tears and ran straight at him," throwing her arms about
his neck and kissing his head.

> He wept as he held his lovely wife. . . .
> And as when the land appears welcome to
> men who are swimming, after Poseidon has
> smashed their strong-built ship on the open
> water . . . so welcome was her husband to
> her as she looked upon him, and she could

not let him go from the embrace of her white arms.

"The gods gave us misery," she tells him, "in jealousy over the thought that we two, always together, should enjoy our youth, and then come to the threshold of old age."

And so they "gladly went together to bed, and their old ritual." And when they "had enjoyed their lovemaking, they took their pleasure in talking, each one telling his story."

This is part of the happy ending.

+   +   +

Here am I in the twentieth century reading something called The Odyssey by someone called Homer. The world I live in is a man-made world that extends all around this aquaterrestrial globe, its surface spotted with cities bound together by networks of roads, of air-lanes, and of sea-lanes. Over a large part of this world most of the population have never seen such vanishing remnants as may still be found of the natural world. In the man-made world people now live like bees in their own architecture, in extensive complexes of cement, macadam, and asphalt. They are supplied with food brought in to them from unknown sources, often halfway around the globe; they are clothed through like procedures; they are protected, educated, trained, indoctrinated, and given medical care by the anonymous powers and procedures of the states to which they respectively belong, socio-political machines that also dispose of their sewage.

The size of the human population is over four thousand million, which means that it is now crowding the planet. Its societies are unstable, so that they are always falling into some kind of disorder, news of which is instantly communicated all around the world, together with pictures. Innumerable airplanes fly from city to city,

144

shunting people around the planet. If there is a break-down at a city called Paris the effects are immediately felt at what once were remote cities, like Tokyo and Buenos Aires. (Odysseus never got so far.)

Here am I, one man in four thousand million, furtively finding a corner by myself where I can read Homer's Odyssey. This literary relict is a product of life around the shores of the Aegean Sea some three thousand years ago. The world was just about un-populated then, almost all wilderness, and the Aegean people didn't even know that they lived on a globe. Their explorations hardly went beyond the vicinity of the eastern Mediterranean, embracing an area that we traverse today in half an hour.

They were not civilized like us, but barbarous, like the precolumbian Indians of North America, like the Vikings, like the Picts and Scots. Their settlements were strongholds on the coast, but set back from the sea-shores so that assailants in their hollow oared boats would have to beach and go inland in order to attack them. A large part of their activity was making war, which they appear to have done by single combat (perhaps quite a few going on simultaneously in one field) with bronze swords, spears, battle-axes, and rocks. Those who won seemingly had no compunctions about chopping up their victims in various ways. They carried off each other's women, and when the lord of a place wasn't around (perhaps because he had gone off to help fetch back someone else's wife) interlopers might move into his domain, devour his substance, and besiege his own wife.

Those who write introductions to The Odyssey for the layman of the twentieth century sometimes tell him just how these ancient people thought and felt. The folks down there in the Aegean three thousand years ago, we laymen are told, thought and felt just like us folks today in Chicago or Ashtabula, in Liverpool or London. Mr. W.H.D. Rouse tells us, "they lived in the country and knew all the sights and sounds of nature

145

and her creatures." (It is an illusion of city men that country men know all the sights and sounds of nature and her creatures.) "They were of a keen intelligence . . .; they pondered the meaning of human life. . . . But there was nothing in them of the prig." (This poses a problem, because T.E. Lawrence has told us that Telemachus was a prig.) "They were not ashamed of enjoying themselves. . . ." (But Telemachus, one recalls, didn't like the way the suitors were enjoying themselves, which must explain why he was a prig.) "Homer sang for a living, as Shakespeare acted for a living. The prince wanted a good story, and he got one. . . ."

Although I daresay this is superficially true, most of it, I really don't think it at all possible for Mr. Rouse or me to get inside the skins of these warrior chieftains, to see with the eyes and hear with the ears of, say, Alcinous, as he sat in the great hall listening to Demodocus sing of the Danaans and the siege of Troy.

Lecturing on the history of the Second World War to students born since it ended, I, who lived through it as an adult, have found how hard it is to show them why we behaved as we did, in that far-off time, by enabling them to see the world as we then saw it, which is so different from the way they see it today. Old attitudes seem incomprehensible to those who have known only such new attitudes as have taken their place; and it is impossible for the new generation to believe in fears that it has never experienced itself. If, then, the present new generation cannot see with the eyes of its elders (even with me still alive to help them), can Mr. Rouse and I really enter freely into the minds of Alcinous and his jolly company of Knights of the Table Round, or whatever we choose to imagine them as being ? (I suspect that Alcinous would not have known what was meant by Mr. Rouse's phrase: "they pondered the meaning of human life.")

No, Mr. Rouse is simply practicing the novelist's art when he sets the scene for a Homer who is exploiting his own talent to make a living—before people who were not ashamed to have fun while they pondered the meaning of human life. We cannot really know what The Odyssey meant to men of 800 B.C. If the auditor's mind is half of it, then The Odyssey as taught at, say, Harvard must be different.

Reading it today, we are uncomfortably aware of all that strikes us quite otherwise than it must have struck the men of its time. Today we cannot regard it as proper for Odysseus, introducing himself to the Phaicians, to say: "I am Odysseus, son of Laertes, known before all men for the study of crafty designs, and my fame goes up to the heavens"—although we know that this kind of boasting is routine in primitive and warlike societies. We are bound to feel uneasy, as well, at the way he makes the most of his sufferings to invite the pity and the gifts of others. Finally, the deaths inflicted on Melanthios and on the delinquent women servants at the end of Book XXII seem repulsively brutal to us, as apparently they did not to those who told the tale.

And yet, these are superficial matters merely. In the end we have to acknowledge something fundamental and imperishable, something that remains for us what it must have been for the men of three thousand years ago, a common essence under the accidentals of manner and attitude. I think of the scene of Odysseus's and Penelope's reunion. And I return to the vision of a normative order toward which men struggle across the wide realms of chaos in which they are plunged, today as three thousand years ago. This is what remains common in the midst of diversity: the vision of a harmonious and orderly society, the fulfillment of lifelong marriage, the regular succession of the generations, the consummation of life in the rhythm of creation, courage and endurance rewarded, the fruits of fidelity realized, the parable of man's striving toward a goal forever the same.

+   +   +

147

The predominant thought of the times through which we are passing is antagonistic to normative visions conceived as having some absolute validity. It is antagonistic to the conception that there is any ideal order that represents what God or nature intended, and that is therefore the proper goal of human striving. It holds that, on the contrary, any order we men establish is our own free invention, without basis in the world of nature on which we impose it. (The denial that there is any order in the universe except what man promulgates, of which Karl Marx may be the first spokesman, is associated with the great urban conglomerations that first developed in the last century; it is associated with thinkers who pass their lives within the man-made environment these conglomerations provide. Bees that had never been outside the hives in which they had been born might, in like fashion, think that they lived in an exclusively bee-made universe.)

The predominant thought of our times also holds that only what is physically demonstrable, and therefore material, represents truth or reality, and it therefore denies any primordial validity to normative ideas or to what Plato called essences. There is, accordingly, no social order that represents a natural propriety for man. If, from Homer through the classical age and two thousand years of Christendom, the ideal of monogamous marriage lasting till death, with its associated ideal of the family group (the Holy Family, in Marx's formulation) —if this ideal has prevailed, it does not follow that whatever was before creation intended it. Plato and Marx upheld other conceptions of propriety, Mohammed another still, and all these conceptions have no greater value or validity than social expediency may give them.

I do not know that this is wrong. What is, however, self-evident is (1) that there is an order in this far-flung cosmos that antedates man's appearance and, if only for that reason, is not of his making; and (2) that there are certain kinds of human behavior, like walking on two legs, that represent a natural propriety for man.

In the solar system, or in the interior of the atom, there is an order that no one would identify as the creation of mankind. In the human mind, as well, there is an order which we call logic, and this order applied to an appreciation of the external environment, matched with the order of the cosmos, has given satisfying if only partial results. The order in the human mind, like the order in the cosmos, does not have its origin in human creation. This leads me to suspect that there must be one natural order, normative by definition.

Does this natural order apply, in terms of propriety, to human behavior ?

Walking on two legs is a natural propriety because it corresponds to the physical structure of the human species. As an additional example, let me take relations between the sexes. In the face of the highly specialized and complementary adaptations of physical structure for the purpose, who can say that the act of physical union, by which new life is engendered, is not in accordance with a natural order, and therefore normative ? Yet there is an intellectual movement in the Anglo-Saxon world today to give homosexual relations the same normative standing as heterosexual. I disqualify myself for the moral judgment of individuals whose bent is toward the former, and who behave accordingly, but surely the evidence of physical adaptation and function is against them when the normative issue is raised. Here we can see a clear design of nature that points to heterosexual relations, rather than homosexual, as representing the natural order.

I could find no such evidence, however, to support the argument that nature intended men and women to enter into monogamous associations for life. Such associations represent only one of a number of possible orderings of relations between the sexes, and while in many societies like our own it has served the socially indispensable purpose of providing for the upbringing of children, societies have been known and can be imagined in which other adequate provision exists for the purpose.

On the basis of my own observation and experience I can say that this ordering of relations between the sexes may provide a satisfaction and fulfillment that I cannot imagine without it. But if some South Sea Islander tells me that he has derived equal satisfaction and fulfillment from having a succession of temporary wives, or several at a time, and if his wives testify to having enjoyed a like satisfaction and fulfillment, then I cannot argue against him or be sure in my own mind that my way has a natural propriety that his does not.

We are all of us born into an existential chaos out of which we struggle to emerge into some order that we may identify with a natural propriety. The lifetime monogamous association between the sexes could conceivably, in the long run, prove to be less well adapted to life in the dense urban conglomerations than some other patterns of relationship, perhaps such a pattern as Plato outlined in The Republic. It does, however, constitute one possible order that, as such, opposes the existential chaos. Because I have come, like so many others, to cherish it, I derive a comforting reassurance before testimony in its favor that goes back as far as three thousand years. Although Homer lived in a society so different from mine that I cannot put myself in his place, here is intimate personal experience that he and I have had in common. The history of the home-coming of Odysseus, and the normative conception that gives it meaning, arouses in me the poignant experience of recognition. The very fact that the recognition takes place across such a wide gulf of time gives me a greater assurance of the stability of the normative vision that Homer and I have in common.

+   +   +

I conceive man's mission on earth to be that of bringing order out of chaos. He is drawn intuitively toward an unknown but pre-existing order, and his creation is really discovery. I offer here two simple examples that have the advantage of being definable in measurable physical terms.

Let us sound a musical tone, say middle-C. If, then, we raise the pitch continously we will suddenly arrive at a tone that seems, somehow, to repeat the one with which we began. Although it is at a higher pitch, and therefore cannot be the same, we still have the subjective impression that the same note has been struck. In our traditional terminology, this tone is the octave of the one with which we began; and if we called the one with which we began C we call this one C too, but C at the interval of an octave higher. (We write it C'.)

Today the growth of scientific discovery has enabled us to explain the affinity we have always apprehended intuitively between the two notes. Our instruments have revealed that each is produced by vibrations of a regular frequency (although so rapid that the ear cannot perceive them as such), and our measurements show that the frequency of the note at the octave is precisely twice that of the original note, that it has two vibrations for every one of the original. (If C is 128 vibrations per second, C' is 256.) Even before we knew this, however, or even knew that there were any vibrations at all, we got a sense of satisfaction out of what seemed to be a repetition of the first note, albeit at a higher pitch. We enjoyed the satisfaction of recognition.

Our original perception of the kinship between the two notes, which preceded our knowledge of the reason for it, was an aesthetic perception. We felt the two notes to be in harmony with each other, although we could not say in what their harmony consisted. All we could say was that there was an indefinable aesthetic satisfaction in hearing them sounded together. Only later did we learn that this satisfaction represented the subjective perception of a basic order in the external universe, an order that could be set forth in mathematical terms.

Again—choose some fundamental tone and then go up the chromatic scale, sounding the successive notes simultaneously with it. In some cases the two sounds will seem to clash with each other, producing what we call a discord. In other cases they will harmonize, and their combination will produce a sense of aesthetic satisfaction. That satisfaction is felt when the fundamental note is sounded with its octave, with its twelfth, with its fifteenth, with its seventeenth, with its nineteenth, etc. The Pythagorean philosophers of the sixth century B.C. already knew that these intervals could be produced by plucking the full length of a stretched cord, then half the length, then a third, then a quarter, etc., so that there was a mathematical relation among them; but it is only in modern times that we have been able to associate this effect of harmony with the fact that the higher notes represent frequencies into which the frequency of the fundamental tone is exactly divisible, without fractional remainders. We perceived the harmony by an intuitive recognition, however, before we knew the mathematical logic by which we were later able to explain it. (It is such an intuitive recognition that unites my mind with Homer's.)

The intervals in question here are those of the so-called harmonic series. If I blow middle-C on my flute, and then progressively intensify the air-pressure, while keeping the fingering for middle-C, the pitch will go up in a shortening series of quantum jumps: first to the octave, then to the twelfth, then to the fifteenth, then to the seventeenth, etc. The same effect can be produced in bowing a violin string: the string vibrates through its whole length to produce the fundamental note, through each of the two halves of its length divided at the middle to produce the octave (double the frequency), through each of the three thirds of its length to produce the twelfth (three times the frequency), through each of the four quarters to produce the fifteenth, etc. The successive tones are separated by quantum jumps that diminish progressively as the series lengthens, until at last the intervals would be infinitesimal if they could still be produced.

The harmony represented by this natural series of frequencies is pervasive in nature, for it is found within every atom, as quantum mechanics have shown. If energy

152

is imparted to an atom by heating it, the atom can absorb that energy only in certain fixed quanta, and consequently it can increase its energy only by quantum jumps that correspond to the harmonic intervals of the violin string. There are two complementary ways of describing this: in this process (1) the electrons around the nucleus of the atom jump into successively wider orbits at intervals that diminish as the series progresses; (2) the electrons increase the frequency of their vibrations by a succession of progressively smaller quantum jumps as the series lengthens out—just as in the case of the harmonic series.

Here, then, is evidence of an order in nature itself that is matched by an order in our own minds, the order in our own minds being represented both by a mathematical logic and by the aesthetic satisfaction we feel when, even without having discovered the mathematical logic, we apprehend it intuitively, finding what we call a harmony in the association of certain tones that we do not find in the association of others. The harmony is in the atom no less than in my flute. It is one Pythagorean harmony pervading the universe.

Now let me take one more example of an a priori order in nature that also has the advantage of associating our subjective impressions with a mathematical logic of which we had no knowledge when our first impressions were formed.

In the Scientific American of September 1965, Martin Gardner reports how the Danish writer and inventor, Piet Hein, set himself to solve a problem that confronted city-planners in Stockholm. The problem was to work out a curved shape, to be fitted into a rectangular city-square, that would be aesthetically satisfying. As Hein put it to himself, it was that of finding the simplest and most pleasing closed curve that would mediate between a rectangle and a simple ellipse, with their mutually clashing tendencies. In the end he worked out what he called a series of superellipses, based on a mathematical formula that need not be expounded here. These curves proved to be strangely satisfying, and the formula has since been adapted to a variety of uses in design. Gardner comments that "one must not confuse the Piet Hein superellipse with the superficially similar potato-shaped curves one often sees, particularly on the face of television sets. These are seldom more than oval patch-works of different kinds of arc, and they lack any simple formula that gives aesthetic unity to the curve."

Here we have the same paradox as in the case of the tonal harmonies and dissonances. A viewer comparing two curves finds one aesthetically satisfying and the other not. Although his intuitive judgment corresponds to the fact that the one is based on a simple mathematical order while the other represents no order, the judgment does not stem from knowledge, even of the fact that there is any mathematical order involved. No one can see the formula as such, or even the fact of a formula. Again, in this example, aesthetic appreciation represents an intuitive discrimination in favor of an order not perceived as such, in opposition to what represents chaos even where it is not known to represent it.*

+   +   +

In the physical universe there is a natural harmony, a harmonious order, that is not always and everywhere completely realized. Alongside it there is also chaos, manifesting itself in disruptions of the order, in accidents, in conflicts and discords of various kinds. Natural order and disorder are to be distinguished, res-pectively, as good and bad, the one representing the objective of all creative advance, the other representing

---

*   Readers who wish to pursue these matters further might look at E. Eugene Helm's "The Vibrating String of the Pythagoreans," in Scientific American of December 1967; my Men and Nations, Princeton, 1962, Chapter I, Section 1; and my Out of Chaos, op. cit., Part One, Chap. IX, and Part V, Chap. IX.

failure. Order represents a natural propriety for the realization of which all being strives.

The natural propriety that is in process of realization throughout the material universe does not exclude the various forms of living being, the plant and animal species. This is clear, for the most part, with respect to virtually every species except our own. Each lives according to an established pattern in which all the forms and procedures are prescribed. Each species of bird typically builds a certain kind of nest peculiar to it, lays a certain number of eggs, cares for its young in certain ways for a certain period, enjoys certain forms of social communion (association, for example, in large flocks, or small, or none at all), engages in certain migratory movements, etc. Some species mate for life and are monogamous, others are polygamous or mate for the season only. My point is that what is proper to each species, its natural propriety, is generally known and established.

To the extent that the action and behavior of the individual represents the a priori pattern for the species, the established order, the human observer of its ways has a sense of harmony and fitness similar to the impression made on him when tones of the harmonic series are sounded together, or to the impression made on him by the superellipse. The swallow coursing in figure-8s over the field of wheat represents the realization, in high degree, of a normative order, a natural propriety. So, in the bilateral symmetry of its form and markings, does the chamois or the prong-horned antelope. Surely this is the meaning of Keats's phrase, "beauty is truth, truth beauty"—if it means anything. For Keats, the figures on the Grecian urn represented a normative order, implicit in the creation, and therefore an ultimate truth.

In the case of our own species, by contrast with all others, we do not yet know what our natural propriety is, what in normative terms are the forms of our society, the relations between our sexes, the modes of our behavior. We are still engaged in a groping evolution toward what, we must hope, will someday emerge as normative for us. In an article called "The Uniqueness of Man,"* Julian Huxley wrote that only man, of all the species, has not yet completed his essential evolution—which is another way of making the point I am making here. This is the dilemma in which we find ourselves, that we do not know or cannot agree on what we are supposed to be, how we are supposed to conduct our lives, what constitutes natural propriety for us.

Still we strive toward a normative order of which we have occasional intuitions. Keats saw it in the Grecian urn; I, like ten thousand generations of my predecessors, see it in The Odyssey.

The Odyssey is a parable of man's striving to emerge from the existential chaos into an ideal order, represented by the Kingdom of Ithaca when it is under the governance of legitimacy. The great poem represents the emergence of man, in consequence of his courage and persistence, from a world of discord into a world of harmony. It is creative, foreshadowing the possibility of a happy end for all mankind.

This is what accounts for the sense of fulfillment with which one finishes The Odyssey.

---

* In the book of that title, London, 1941.

THE PASSING OF ARTHUR

Death is the theme of <u>Hamlet</u>: the death of a once hopeful social order, the death of those who had served it, at last the death of friends and foes alike in a general ruin.

In the history of the Greek expedition against Troy, too, death plays the final role. When the normative order of the day is broken by the adultery of Paris and Helen, anarchy is loosed upon the world. Only Odysseus escapes, after twenty years of travail, from the general ruin. And Helen, at the end, might truly have said that her affair with Paris had brought about the collapse of a whole world, leaving the closing scene littered with lifeless bodies like dead ants about a colony struck by cataclysm.

At the end of Sir Thomas Malory's <u>Le Morte d'Arthur</u>, when Launcelot returns as a refugee from the ruins of the Arthurian order to his last interview with Arthur's queen, in the convent where she has taken asylum, she can truthfully say to those who attend her: "Through this man and me hath all this war been wrought, and the death of the noblest knights of the world; for through our love that we have loved together is my most noble lord slain." Where once the order of the Round Table had sustained the hopes of mankind, death dominates the scene—as on the battlefield of Troy, as at the Court of Denmark when the slow drums of Fortinbras beat the last retreat.

+   +   +

This history of Arthur and his realm, like the history of Troy and the history of Hamlet's Denmark, belongs to the world's dark ages. Men encompassed by anarchy strive to maintain or impose a normative order,

159

only to fail in the end because of the Old Adam within them.

The setting of Arthur's effort is Europe after the collapse of the Roman order. It has returned to the wilderness, returned to the pristine condition that, as Hobbes put it, is one "of war of everyone against everyone. . . . No arts; no letters; no society; and which is worst of all, continual fear and danger of violent death; and the life of man, solitary, poor, nasty, brutish, and short." In the dark age that follows the collapse of the Roman civilization we have the story of two heroic attempts, both ultimately defeated, to establish a civilized order. One is that of Charlemagne and his paladins, the other that of Arthur and his fellowship of the Round Table.

Just as we have no historical record of Agammemnon or Priam, both of whom undoubtedly lived, so we have none of Arthur, although Charlemagne has a double existence, historical as well as legendary. The Arthurian epic represents some former body of fact that has come down to us only in the form of a legendary residue left in the collective memory. As with all legends, the matrix of the events that are recounted is a normative order that the individual actors are called upon to fulfill. It is commonly revealed to them by supernatural signs, by miracles and magic; and the test of legitimacy, applied to the conduct of the struggling actors, is in its fulfillment.

All this is well represented by the circumstances in which Arthur becomes King of England with the mission of bringing order to the anarchic world of his day. Throughout this history he represents the "humility and patience" without which men may not overcome. (This is a normative concept identified with Christianity and therefore not to be found in the Homeric world.)

The boy Arthur, as we first meet him, is content to be no more than the humble person he has always supposed himself to be, the son of a knight called Sir Ector and squire to Sir Ector's older son, Sir Kay.

Because the throne of England had been left vacant upon the death of King Uther Pendragon, the realm is sinking into anarchy, "for every lord that was mighty of men made him strong, and many weened to have been king." Arthur did not concern himself with such high matters, and consequently was ignorant even of the supernatural provision that had been made for identifying the one among the contending lords who was to be the new king. Attending jousts in London as Sir Kay's squire, he was unaware of the fact that a sword in a stone, which he had noted casually in a churchyard, was inscribed with letters that read: "Whoso pulleth out this sword of this stone . . . is rightwise king born of all England." He was unaware of the fact that all the great lords had been essaying in vain to pull it out. One Sunday morning, however, Sir Kay was careless enough to leave his own sword behind at their lodgings when he had gone to the jousts. Arthur, having been sent back to fetch it, found nobody home and the lodgings locked. Happily, then, he bethought him of the sword he had seen in the churchyard. Hurrying there, he took it from the stone and ran with it to Sir Kay.

The amazement and confusion of Sir Ector and Sir Kay were what might have been expected. When they were finally convinced that it really was Arthur who had drawn the sword from the stone, Sir Ector solemnly announced to him that it was he who must be king of all England in succession to Uther Pendragon. A dismayed Arthur could respond only by asking: "Wherefore I, and for what cause ?" Then, when Sir Ector and Sir Kay actually knelt down before him, he exclaimed in distress: "Alas, my own dear father and brother, why kneel ye to me ?" Finally, when Sir Ector revealed that he was not Arthur's real father, but his foster father only, Arthur "made great doole." It was only many months later that he and all England learned, from Merlin, that the test of the sword in the stone accorded with the legitimacy of his succession as the son, in fact, of Uther Pendragon.

From this point on Arthur bears the lifetime burden of a mission he had never sought. Throughout the tragic history of his subsequent efforts to carry out that mission, however, he allows no consideration of self to stand in the way, but acts ever with the "humility and patience" of the boy who had drawn the sword from the stone after the greatest lords of England had failed. With Hamlet he might at any time have said:

> The time is out of joint; O cursed spite,
> That ever I was born to set it right !

And in the end, do what he may, no more than Hamlet will he succeed. The tragic basis of our human life is that our normative visions exceed our capacity to realize them.

+   +   +

Just as Paris enjoyed an illicit union with Menelaus's queen, Helen, which resulted in the destruction of half the world, so it was to pass that Sir Launcelot du Lake, Arthur's best friend and worthiest subject, would have an illicit union with Arthur's queen, Guenever, which would have like consequences.

There is never any doubt that, in fulfillment of the new order struggling to be born, Guenever's appointed role is that of Arthur's queen; for it is her father, King Leodegrance, who bestows upon Arthur the dowery of the Round Table, which is to be both the symbol and the means of his mission, just as the cross is both the symbol and the means of Christ's mission. It is through the sworn fellowship of the knights who are to occupy its hundred and fifty places that Arthur must attempt to overcome the moral anarchy of the world and establish, in its place, the normative order of the chivalric code; "for men may no time overcome humility and patience, therefore was the Round Table founded."

Launcelot and Arthur are the two equal heroes of Malory's tale. Launcelot, however, is marked by personal ambition as Arthur is not, although his ambition is not for power or riches but simply to be the best knight in the world. We might ask whether this means that he wants to be the best in moral worth or best in prowess. Within the normative framework of Malory's tale, however, the two kinds of excellence are not separable. It is only by moral purity, in thought and conduct alike, that a knight can hope to achieve supremacy in the field. Launcelot's ambition, therefore, is nothing if not creditable; although it is an ambition that would not have occurred to anyone so lacking in self-regard as the lad who would have been content to remain Sir Kay's squire.

From his first coming to the fellowship of the Round Table Launcelot proves himself the best in prowess, passing all other knights in tournaments and jousts and deeds of arms. "Wherefore Queen Guenever had him in great favour above all other knights, and in certain he loved the queen again above all other ladies and damosels of his life."

This love between Launcelot and the wife of his cherished lord, seemingly so innocent when we first hear of it, is the canker in the bud of the order that is struggling to be born. Because of it, however, Launcelot will consistently refuse to have ado with any other lady or damosel. By a fidelity in itself noble, he will resist all the temptations of the sort that will come his way throughout his life, so that the enduring love of Launcelot and Guenever stands at the highest rank among the love-stories of the world. It is a story of fidelity and infidelity together.

What had been foreordained, however, no less than the accession of Arthur to the throne of England, was that Launcelot would engender a son, Galahad, who should realize the greatest achievement of chivalry, and that he should engender him upon Elaine, the daughter of King Pelles of Corbin. In terms of the propriety established by the powers that create the design to be realized, Elaine was the one to whom Launcelot owed the lifelong fidelity that he gave, instead, to another man's wife. In consequence of this single failure, the failure of the best knight in the world to resist the seductions of the flesh, Arthur's mission will fail and the whole world that was being created through the agency of the Round Table will at last collapse in universal death and disaster.

+   +   +

Riding in quest of adventure one day, Launcelot came to the town of Corbin, where Elaine was imprisoned in a tower by an enchantment according to which she could never be freed except by the best knight in the world. Launcelot, having freed her, "thought she was the fairest lady of the world, but if it were Queen Guenever." He was then invited by Elaine and her father, King Pelles, to be their guest in the castle of Corbin, where the Holy Grail appeared to the three of them as they sat down to their repast. This is symbolic, for it is through the consequences of a union between Launcelot and Elaine that, as has been foreordained, the future quest of the Grail will be achieved.

"And fain would King Pelles have found the mean to have had Sir Launcelot to have lain by his daughter, fair Elaine. And for this intent: the king knew well that Sir Launcelot should get a child upon his daughter, the which should be named Sir Galahad the good knight, . . . and by him the Holy Greal should be achieved."

A member of the Pelles household who practices enchantments, Dame Brisen, now tells the King: "Sir, wit ye well Sir Launcelot loveth no lady in the world but all only Queen Guenever; and therefore work ye by my counsel, and I shall make him to lie with you daughter, and he shall not wit but that he lieth with Queen Guenever." So, by conspiracy and enchantment, Launcelot spends the night in a neighboring castle and begets Galahad upon Elaine under the impression that he is keeping an assignation with Arthur's queen.

When day breaks, ending the enchantment, Launce-lot learns of the deception that has been practiced upon him, and in a moment of horror draws his sword to slay Elaine. "Then this fair lady Elaine skipped out of her bed all naked, and kneeled down afore Sir Launcelot, and said: Fair courteous knight, come of king's blood, I require you have mercy upon me, and as thou art renowned the most noble knight of the world, slay me not, for I have in my womb him by thee that shall be the most noble knight of the world." Launcelot, who throughout this history is rarely able to resist any appeal to his compassion, forgives her and, as he takes his departure, she says to him: "My lord Sir Launcelot, I beseech you see me as soon as you may, for I have obeyed me unto the prophecy that my father told me. And by his commandment to fulfil this prophecy I have given the greatest riches and the fairest flower that ever I had, and that is my maidenhood that I shall never have again; and therefore, gentle knight, owe me your good will." But Launcelot, to the very end, is as a man possessed. There can never be any question, for him, of making a choice between the mother of his son and the wife of his liege lord.

+   +   +

After the birth of Galahad there is a second union between Launcelot and Elaine, also contrived by conspiracy and enchantment. Still in the hope of making him her own, she comes to a great feast given in Camelot, where she is warmly received by King Arthur and the knights of the Round Table. And when she "was brought unto Queen Guenever either made other good cheer by countenance, but nothing with hearts." Launcelot, in acute embarrassment, is cold to her, whereupon Dame Brisen repeats the trickery of the first encounter. The Queen, who has bidden him come to her chamber that night, awaits him in vain, for Dame Brisen has led him, instead, to Elaine's chamber, where he lies with her all night under the impression, again, that she is Guenever. Guenever, however, surprises him in Elaine's chamber and, in her fury, cries out: "False traitor knight that thou art, look thou never abide in my court, and avoid my chamber, and not so hardy, thou false traitor knight

165

that thou art, that ever thou come in my sight." This is too much for Launcelot's sanity, which suddenly gives way altogether. Clad only in his shirt, he leaps from the window and runs away wild.

Thereupon Elaine turns to Guenever and says: "Madam, ye are greatly to blame for Sir Launcelot, for now have ye lost him, for I saw and heard by his countenance that he is mad for ever. Alas, madam, ye do great sin, and to yourself great dishonour, for ye had a lord of your own, and therefore it is your part to love him; for there is no queen in this world hath such another king as ye have. And if ye were not I might have the love of my lord Sir Launcelot; and cause I have to love him for he had my maidenhood, and by him I have born a fair son, and his name is Galahad, and he shall be in his time the best knight of the world."

Nowhere in the tale, whether explicitly or by implication, is there any attribution of villainy to either of the two women who make their respective claims on Launcelot's love and loyalty. Guenever is not a wicked enchantress like Morgan le Fay, but rather a very human being who is utterly ruled by passion and posses-siveness. Elaine, on the other hand, has right on her side when she rebukes Guenever, for Guenever in the role of Eve has drawn Launcelot from obedience to a foreordained order, thereby re-enacting the Fall of Man in the Garden of Eden. But she and Launcelot alike are the victims of a mutual passion that neither has the strength to master. So it is that all three parties to this triangle of Launcelot, Guenever, and Elaine are proper objects of compassion. This is also the case, as we shall see, when it comes to that associated triangle of Guenever, Arthur, and Launcelot. Here human beings are struggling vainly in the toils of passions that drive them to break the bounds of the normative order.

For over two years Launcelot, now out of his wits, runs naked in the wilderness, living on berries and roots, while the best knights of the Round Table, at the behest of the King and Queen alike, seek him far and wide. Then "by adventure he came to the city of Corbin, where Dame Elaine was. . . . And so when he was entered into the town he ran through the town to the castle; and then all the young men of that city ran after Sir Launcelot, and there they threw turves at him, and gave him many sad strokes." But the knights and squires of the castle come to his rescue and bring him inside. Here he is given "clothes to his body, and straw underneath him, and a little house." As a dangerous madman, however, he is kept confined, and although every day the people of the castle would "throw him meat, and set him drink,. . . there was but few would bring him meat to his hands."

Inevitably the day comes when Elaine sees the fool of the castle, which is what Launcelot has become for the servitors, and recognizes him. Then by the grace that is in the Holy Grail, which once before had descended upon Launcelot and Elaine in the castle of Corbin, he is at last cured of his madness.

A broken and defeated man now, exiled from Arthur's court and forever banished from the presence of the woman he loves, he settles down to live with the mother of his son in the nearby castle of Bliant, no longer as Sir Launcelot du Lake, no longer as the best knight in the world, but as The Ill-made Knight, Le Chevaler Mal Fet—translated by Malory as "the knight that hath trespassed."

Elaine, asked by Launcelot to set up house with him, responds like Ruth in the Old Testament: "Sir, I will live and die with you, and only for your sake; and if my life might not avail you and my death might avail you, wit you well I would die for your sake. . . . And where ye be, my lord Sir Launcelot, doubt ye not but I will be with you with all the service that I may do."

The Chevaler Mal Fet now has a shield made himself, however, "all of sable, and a queen crowned in the midst, all of silver, and a knight clene armed kneeling afore her." And every day once he would "look toward the realm of Logris, where King Arthur and Queen Guenever was. And then he would fall upon a weeping as his heart should to brast."

All this while Guenever, moved by the same longing, and desolate at having driven Launcelot from her, has the knights of the Round Table out seeking him throughout the realm of Britain. In this she is at one with King Arthur, who longs for the recovery and return of his best friend and the finest knight of his fellowship—not, as he believes, an ill-made knight, but the best knight in all the world.

So the time comes at last, as come it must, when Launcelot's brother Sir Ector de Maris and Sir Percivale find him in his retirement with Elaine, discover his identity, and reveal to him that, so far from being unwelcome at King Arthur's court, "King Arthur and all his knights, and in especial Queen Guenever" have been sorrowing at his absence. Launcelot, once he knows this, agrees without hesitation to return to the court at the forthcoming feast of Pentecost. Elaine and his son are all but forgotten in this moment of his restoration. "And when Sir Launcelot should depart Dame Elaine made great sorrow. My lord, Sir Launcelot, said Dame Elaine, at this same feast of Pentecost shall your son and mine, Galahad, be made knight, for he is fully now fifteen winter old. Do as ye list, said Sir Launcelot; God give him grace to prove a good knight."

Upon Launcelot's return there was rejoicing in Camelot. First "Queen Guenever wept as she should have died." Then she "made great cheer. O Jesu, said King Arthur, I marvel for what cause ye, Sir Launcelot, went out of your mind. I and many others deem it was for the love of fair Elaine, the daughter of King Pelles, by whom ye are noised that ye have gotten a child, and his name is Galahad, and men say he shall do marvels. My lord, said Sir Launcelot, if I did any folly I have that I sought. And therewithal the king spake no more. But all Sir Launcelot's kin knew for whom he went out of his mind."

168

+   +   +

<u>Le Morte d'Arthur</u> is not a unified literary struc-
ture like <u>Hamlet</u> and <u>The Odyssey</u>. It consists of a
number of interwoven histories, each of which involves
numberless anecdotes of chivalric adventure told for
their own sake and unnecessary to the argument. It is
as much a whole literature as it is a single piece of
literature. However, although moving along no direct
path of development, digressing constantly and sometimes
seeming to lose itself in irrelevancies, it proves in the
end to have an underlying unity that belies the surface
of diversity and confusion.

One of the histories it relates is, as we have seen,
that of Sir Launcelot's ambition to be the best knight in
the world, and the bearing on its realization of his
trespass. Another is the superficially similar history of
Sir Tristam de Liones, the only other knight in a class
with Launcelot, and his lifelong love-affair with La Beale
Isoud, the wife of his own liege lord, King Mark of
Cornwall. Tristam, like Launcelot, goes out of his wits
and runs naked in the wilderness because of a misunder-
standing with La Beale Isoud; and like Launcelot he
endures a loveless union with another devoted woman,
Isoud La Blanche Mains. King Mark, in the Tristam
history, serves as a foil to King Arthur in the history
of Launcelot, for he is craven and treacherous, at last
killing Tristam from behind, so that the Tristam-Isoult
story, while running parallel to the Launcelot-Guenever
story, also presents a contrast to it that brings it into
higher relief.

Another history, that of the quest of the Holy
Grail, while it constitutes a crucial chapter in the
history of Launcelot, has its own completeness and
integrity. Above all it has a tone of its own, predomi-
nantly religious. It is full of mystical happenings and
magic signs, of occult experiences in wayside chapels, of
demons in disguise offering temptation, of hermits
offering absolution or prophecy. Here, more than any-
where else, the inner state of each actor, in terms of

Christian grace, is the condition of his outward achievement.

In the end, however, all these distinct histories are elements in the one great tragedy denoted by the title given Malory's work. Moving together or separately through the lifetime of a whole generation, they combine in leading to the final scene, like the final scene of Hamlet, that of a battlefield at nightfall in which Arthur lies dying amid the heaped-up corpses of those who had constituted the fellowship of the Round Table—with only Sir Bedivere left alive, like Horatio, to draw his breath in pain while he bears witness to future generations of these terrible happenings.

To the extent that the story of the quest of the Grail is dominated by mystical symbolism, revealing the intrusiveness of the heavenly powers, the element of basic human nature essential to heroism and tragedy is reduced. The Grail itself, which contains the blood gathered by Joseph of Arimethea from Christ as he bled on the cross, appears to represent something like the salvation from our earthly bonds promised in the Second Coming. It is a form of the Christ himself, for it contains his presence. The achievement of the Grail, reserved for Galahad alone, is the achievement of union with Christ in the heavenly kingdom.

Galahad, the incarnation not of a relative but of an absolute perfection, thereby represents but a denatured man. He is without inner conflicts, which is to say that he is without an inner life as we real human beings experience it. If we others are, by definition, the fallen creatures of Christian tradition, then Galahad may be said to lack the common humanity that Christ himself assumed, and which enables us to identify ourselves with him. For Christ did have an inner life as we know it in ourselves, he did have inner conflicts, he did have to steel himself against temptations. At one point, facing the imminent prospect of his martyrdom, he experienced the fear that prompted him to ask of God the Father: "If it be possible, let this cup pass from me." Galahad, by constrast, never knows fear. On the cross Christ at one moment lost his faith, crying out: "My God, my God, why hast thou forsaken me ?" Such human weakness is unknown to Galahad. Moreover, because Galahad appears immune to all temptation, he cannot be credited either with the experience of struggling against it or the merit of overcoming it. In the implicit contrast between the unhuman Galahad and his very human father, the imperfect stands above the perfect in our eyes. This paradox, as we shall see, is brought out with over-whelming effect at the culminating moment in Launcelot's life.

As must be true of all extensive bodies of legend—partly because of the way they develop and ramify over the generations, perhaps also because they embody standard archetypal patterns of the collective un-conscious—certain motifs and themes are repeated in varying forms. We have already seen this in the parallel histories of Launcelot and Tristam. Le Morte d'Arthur contains a similar contrasting parallel in the events by which the respective missions of Arthur and Galahad are inaugurated.

On the day of Pentecost in the year A.D. 454, the foreordained date on which the quest of the Holy Grail was to begin, the company at King Arthur's court dis-covered a great stone floating in the nearby river, and sticking therein a sword with letters on its pommel that read: "Never shall man take me hence, but only he by whose side I ought to hang, and he shall be the best knight of the world." When King Arthur had seen the letters "he said unto Sir Launcelot: Fair sir, this sword ought to be yours, for I am sure ye be the best knight of the world." But Launcelot, knowing his trespass, declined to take hold of it, saying: "Certes, sir, it is not my sword."

Other knights, less conscious of any blemish in themselves, essayed to draw the sword from the stone and failed.

At the noonday feast that follows this incident, Galahad makes his first entry to the court of King Arthur, calmly seating himself at the Round Table in the seat known as the Siege Perilous, never before occupied because only the knight "that shall pass all other knights" might sit in it with impunity. After the feast he is taken to the sword in the stone. The King tells him that "right good knights have essayed and failed" to draw it out; to which Galahad replies: "Sir, that is no marvel, for this adventure is not theirs but mine"; whereupon he lifts the sword from the stone and slips it into an empty scabbard he has brought along for the purpose. Again, recalling how Sir Kay's unpretending squire had drawn the sword from the stone in the London churchyard a generation earlier, we have the combination of a parallel and a contrast.

Immediately after Galahad has taken the sword from the stone and packed it into his scabbard, a lady on a white palfrey comes riding down the river and, weeping, addresses Sir Launcelot. "How your great doing is changed sith this day in the morn. Damosel, why say you so ? said Launcelot. I say you sooth, said the damosel, for ye were this day the best knight of the world, but who should say so now, he should be a liar, for there is now one better than ye, and well it is proved by the adventure of the sword whereto ye durst not set to your hand; and that is the change and leaving of your name. Wherefore I make unto you a remembrance, that ye shall not ween from henceforth that ye be the best knight of the world. As touching unto that, said Launcelot, I know well I was never the best. Yes, said the damosel, that were ye, and are yet, of any sinful man of the world."

That evening Sir Galahad, Sir Launcelot, and all the other knights of the Round Table depart on the quest of the Holy Grail, each to take "the way that him best liked." Behind them they leave a desolate king and an inconsolable queen, for this is the end of the first and the best fellowship of the Round Table. Arthur knows how few of his knights will return.

If one theme of the quest is the apotheosis of Galahad, a complementary theme is the chastening of Launcelot. At one juncture Launcelot, who has never before been overcome, meets a knight whom he does not recognize as his son until after the knight has overthrown him and continued on his way. When he does come into the presence of the Grail he is rendered unable to see it and powerless to move. After the Grail is gone he exclaims: "My sin and my wickedness have brought me unto great dishonour. For when I sought worldly adventures for worldly desires, I ever achieved them and had the better in every place, and never was I discomfit in no quarrel, were it right or wrong. And now I take upon me the adventures of holy things, and now I see and understand that mine old sin hindereth me and shameth me, so that I had no power to stir nor speak when the holy blood appeared afore me."

He then finds a hermit to shrive him, confessing to him how "he had loved a queen unmeasurably and out of measure long. And all my great deeds of arms that I have done, I did for the most part for the queen's sake, and for her sake would I do battle were it right or wrong; and never did I battle all only for God's sake, but for to win worship and to cause me to be the better beloved, and little or no I thanked God for it."

All men bear the canker of Original Sin, but not all acknowledge it. Launcelot, like no other character in the Arthurian legends, is akin to the Hamlet who cries out: "I could accuse me of such things that it were better my mother had never borne me." Throughout Malory's history it is evident that the element of what he calls lechery is a major part of the love that Launcelot and Guenever enjoy between them, and this element has never been accorded legitimacy in the Christian tradition. In the Christian tradition it is what represents Original Sin. However that may be, only those who are guided by a normative ideal, who aspire to perfection, are fully conscious of their failings. The hermit tells Launcelot that God has given him "discretion to know good from evil." He then exacts from him a promise "that ye will never come in that queen's fellowship." We shall see that it will be beyond Launcelot's strength to keep this promise, that the Queen and the enjoyment she represents for him cannot be banished from his thoughts.

Later he is told by another religious man that, seek the Grail as he may, "though it were here ye shall have no power to see it no more than a blind man should see a bright sword, and that is long on your sin, and else ye were more abler than any man living." He now abjures both meat and wine, and takes to wearing a hair shirt in a vain attempt to subdue the Old Adam in him.

At last, after many months and many marvels, Launcelot is accorded the grace of seeing the Holy Grail through the open door of a chamber into which he is forbidden to enter. When, irresistably drawn by the vision, he attempts to enter anyway he is smitten so that he falls into a swoon, lying like a dead man for four and twenty days to match the four and twenty years that he has, by now, been in his sin.

His own personal quest thus ended, Launcelot returns to Camelot "where he found King Arthur and the queen. But many of the knights of the Round Table were slain and destroyed, more than half."

The actual achievement of the quest for the Grail is reserved for Sir Galahad, with Sir Percivale and Sir Bors in attendance, the first two having never been sullied by carnal relations with any woman, and the third having remained chaste after a single lapse. The Savior himself appears to Galahad and delivers to him the Grail for removal out of Britain to the city of Sarras near Babylon. Accompanied by Percivale and Bors, Galahad proceeds to do this. He is then carried up to Heaven by a multitude of angels, to be joined with Jesus Christ, after which a hand descends from Heaven to take up the Holy Grail as well, since which "was there never man so hardy to say that he had seen the Sangreal."

Percivale then enters into a nearby hermitage,

where he leads a holy life until his death a year and two months later, after which Sir Bors returns across land and sea to the court of King Arthur, where he makes known the end of the quest.

+ + +

The quest and achievement of the Holy Grail represent the high point in the great undertaking of the Arthurian order to rise above the evil of the world, to transcend the penalty of Original Sin. What remains is a long decline to the tragic end.

The failure of Launcelot is now confirmed beyond any hope of his again realizing his aspiration to be the best knight in the world. Had he not been "in his privy thoughts and in his mind so set inwardly to the queen as he was in seeming outward to God," Malory tells us, "there had been no knight passed him in the quest of the Sangreal." Now he "began to resort unto Queen Guenever again, and forgat the promise and the perfection that he made in the quest. . . . Ever his thoughts were privily on the queen, and so they loved together more hotter than they did toforehand, and had such privy draughts together, that many in the court spake of it."

After the rarefied mysticism of the chapters on the quest of the Grail, the reader finds relief in the return to the level of our common humanity. At that level, Guenever has no counterpart in literature except Shakespeare's Cleopatra, whom she resembles in some ways. Like the ageing Cleopatra, who has no legitimate hold on Antony, she gives way to transports of jealousy when Launcelot, to protect her from scandal, tries to disguise their relationship in public, making an ostentatious display of chivalric attention to other ladies of the court. It is in vain that he tells her: "If I had not had my privy thoughts to return to your love again as I do, I had seen as great mysteries as ever saw my son Galahad, outher Percivale, or Sir Bors."

While he spoke "the queen stood still and let Sir Launcelot say what he would. And when he had all said she brast out on weeping, and so she sobbed and wept a great while. And when she might speak she said: Launcelot, now I well understand that thou art a false recreant knight and a common lecher, and lovest and holdest other ladies, and by me thou hast disdain and scorn." (How many times has this scene, heartbreaking for both parties, been played in every generation of mankind !) Finally, at the full pitch of her fury, as had happened once before, she charges him to leave the court and never appear at it again.

A day comes, however, when a champion is needed to fight for the Queen's life, and then Launcelot returns to a rescue followed by a reconciliation. "And ever the queen beheld Sir Launcelot, and wept so tenderly that she sank almost to the ground for sorrow that he had done to her so great goodness where she shewed him great unkindness."

+   +   +

What follows is another incident to arouse the jealousy of the Queen, an incident that has in it an echo of the disappointed love that the mother of Galahad, long since dead, had had for Launcelot. On his way to a tourney Launcelot, out of pure compassion for another Elaine, this one the fair maiden of Astolat, agrees to wear her token when he enters the jousts. The love of the second Elaine for Launcelot is just as selfless and even more frustrated than that of the first, for it is never to be consumated. When Launcelot is wounded at the tourney she nurses him back to strength, doing "ever her diligent labour night and day unto Sir Launcelot, that there was never child nor wife more meeker to her father and husband than was that fair maiden of Astolat."

After many weeks, when Launcelot, at last recovered, is ready to leave her father's home and return to the court, where he will again have to face the wrath of an unhappy queen, she says to him: "My lord, Sir Launcelot, now I see ye will depart; now fair knight and courteous knight, have mercy upon me, and suffer me not to die for thy love. What would ye that I did ? said Sir Launcelot. I would have you to my husband, said Elaine. Fair damosel, I thank you, said Sir Launcelot, but truly, said he, I cast me never to be wedded man. Then, fair knight, said she, will ye be my paramour ? Jesu defend me, said Sir Launcelot, for then I rewarded your father and your brother full evil of their great goodness."

The rest of the story is well known through Tennyson's poem: how Elaine, refusing food or drink, pined away and died; how her body clad in rich clothes and placed in a fair bed was floated on a barge down the Thames to King Arthur's court at Westminster; how, when it arrived, a letter was found in her hand avowing her love for Launcelot while affirming that "a clene maiden I died"; and how the King, the Queen, and all the knights wept for pity at it.

The Queen, who in wild anger at his relationship with Elaine had refused to speak to Launcelot since his return, now spoke to him at last. "Ye might have shewed her, said the queen, some bounty and gentleness that might have preserved her life."

+   +   +

The passion of physical desire that still, after so many years, dominates the lives of Launcelot and the Queen is revealed again in an incident that now follows. A pitiful knight called Sir Meliagrance, who has for years been secretly obsessed with desire for Guenever, takes advantage of her going off a-maying with a few unarmed knights to kidnap her and carry her off to his castle. Launcelot, immediately informed, succeeds in reaching the castle before she suffers any violation. Thereupon, Meliagrance in a panic seeks the Queen's forgiveness and pleads for her intercession with Launcelot, which she grants. The whole party then agree to spend the night at the castle of Meliagrance as his guests, the knights of the Queen, who had been wounded in the attempt to defend her, to be bedded down for her protection outside the door of her bed-chamber.

That night "Sir Launcelot took his sword in his hand, and privily went to a place where he had espied a ladder toforehand, and that he took under his arm, and bare it through the garden, and set it up to the window, and there anon the queen was ready to meet him. And they made either to other their complaints of many diverse things, and then Sir Launcelot wished that he might have come in to her. Wit ye well, said the queen, I would as fain as ye, that ye might come in to me. Would ye, madam, said Sir Launcelot, with your heart that I were with you? Yea, truly, said the queen. Now shall I prove my might, said Sir Launcelot, for your love; and then he set his hands upon the bars of iron, and he pulled at them with such a might that he brast them clene of the stone walls, and therewithal one of the bars of iron cut the brawn of his hands throughout to the bone; and then he leapt into the chamber to the queen. Make ye no noise, said the queen, for my wounded knights lie here fast by me. So, to pass upon this tale, Sir Launcelot went unto bed with the queen, and he took no force of his hurt hand, but took his pleasance until it was in the dawning of the day: and wit ye well he slept not but watched, and when he saw his time that he might tarry no longer he took his leave and departed at the window, and put it together as well as he might again."

That morning Meliagrance, discovering blood from Launcelot's wounded hand on the Queen's bed-clothes, makes a formal accusation against her that one of the wounded knights outside her door has lain with her. The end of the matter is that, to avenge the Queen's honor, Launcelot escapes from a trap Meliagrance sets for him and kills him in single combat.

+   +   +

Launcelot has formally saved Guenever's honor. But there is no question in his mind that his own honor has long been lost, and with it the hope that he had once lived for of being the best knight in all the world. Those who are ignorant of his guilty secret may be under the illusion that he is the best knight, but he himself knows better. He knows himself to be a man who is living a lie, and he is only too aware of the danger that at any time the lie may become publicly known.

At last the dreaded day comes when it seems to him that it must become known. There was a Hungarian knight called Sir Urre who had for years borne upon his body seven wounds that could never be healed except by the touch of the best knight in the world. In search of that healing, his mother had for seven years had him carried in a horse-litter through "all lands christened," exposing himself to the touch of all the best knights wherever he went, and all to no avail. The last countries to which he came were Scotland and then England, finally arriving at Carlisle, where King Arthur was holding his court.

On the meadow of Carlisle, then, King Arthur assembled "all the kings, dukes, and earls, and all noble knights of the Round Table that were there that time present." Arthur undertook to search Sir Urre's wounds first, "not presuming upon me [as he told Sir Urre's mother] that I am so worthy to heal your son by my deeds, but I will courage other men of worship to do as I will do."

King Arthur fails as he had known he would, and after him successively a hundred and ten knights who are present, including even Sir Bors de Ganis, the only survivor of the three who had achieved the Grail. At last no one is left but Sir Launcelot, who is now brought forward. Here begins an agonizing scene in which Launcelot, confronted with the assurance of King Arthur and the others that he, being the best knight in the world, will succeed where they failed, tries by all means to avoid the ultimate humiliation of the failure that, because of his trespass, he has to anticipate. Finally King Arthur tells him: "Ye shall not choose, for I will command you to do as we all have done."

Launcelot, with no alternative left, now kneels down to do what he must, even though it will cost him the false reputation on which his standing with the others depends. At the same time he says, speaking silently: "Thou blessed Father, Son, and Holy Ghost, I beseech thee of mercy, that my simple worship and honesty be saved, and thou blessed Trinity, thou mayst give power to heal this sick knight by thy great virtue and grace of thee, but, good lord, never of myself." Amid the general silence, then, he begins to apply his fingers to Sir Urre's wounds—"and forthwithal the wounds fair healed, and seemed as they had been whole a seven year."

When the multitude of observers, after a moment, beheld and knew what had happened, the silence broke. Then there was sudden wild rejoicing, with all present including King Arthur falling to their knees in thanksgiving. "And ever," Malory writes, "Sir Launcelot wept as he had been a child that had been beaten."

For Launcelot, and for the reader himself, this unexpected triumph comes like another redemption after the fall of man.

+   +   +

The episode in Le Morte d'Arthur that I have just recounted, providing the most exalted moment in the whole history, comes immediately before the final tragedy; just as the most exalted moment in Hamlet, when Hamlet himself attains a serenity he had never known before, comes in that tragedy's penultimate scene. Here on earth below, where life goes on past all moments of triumph or defeat, exaltation can sometimes be experienced but never sustained. In the long history of Arthur's failure the end is now at hand.

The fellowship of the Round Table, like every

human community, had always had an element of factionalism, whether latent or overt. The reader is aware, for example, that Sir Gawaine, Sir Agravaine, Sir Gaheris, Sir Gareth, and Sir Mordred, associated together as the sons of King Lot of Orkney by King Arthur's sister Queen Morgawse, have, in addition to the bonds of family loyalty that unite them, a sort of wordliness and a pride of position that distinguish them from the family of King Ban of Brittany: Launcelot, his brother Ector de Maris, their nephews Lionel and Bors. Here are latent possibilities of jealousy that first manifest themselves in two of the five brothers after the scene of Launcelot's redemption, and because of it.

Now, writes Malory, "it befell a great anger and unhap that stinted not till the flower of chivalry of all the world was destroyed and slain." For "Sir Agravaine and Sir Mordred had ever a privy hate unto the queen Dame Guenever and to Sir Launcelot, and daily and nightly they ever watched upon Sir Launcelot."

It should be noted that the love affair between Launcelot and Guenever, now of at least a quarter century's duration, had for years been an open secret at King Arthur's court. (Their knowledge of it would certainly have contributed to any resentment that Agravaine and Mordred felt at Launcelot's triumph on the field of Carlisle.) One may speculate that Arthur, himself, had remained ignorant of it out of the simplicity of his character; or one may speculate more plausibly that considerations of statesmanship had led him deliberately to pretend ignorance of it. He would have seen clearly that his civilizing mission, imposed on him when he first drew the sword from the stone, would be fatally prejudiced if ever he had to take cognisance of his wife's adultery with Launcelot and, in consequence, do something about it. Immediately the credit of the court and the Round Table would have been destroyed by open scandal, his own authority would have been lost, the best of his knights would have been thrown into opposition with all his kinsmen and partisans, anarchy would have consumed the chivalric fellowship that had been created to put it down. So wise parents sometimes pretend not to have seen acts of misbehavior by their children because otherwise the consequences would be disproportionate. In like fashion there have been wise women who have pretended to be unaware of their hus- bands' infidelities. In the world as it is, in which we poor mortals can so rarely live up to our normative standards, we can sometimes save these standards only by pretending that, in fact, we all do. A marriage may be more important than an act of adultery that would break it up if brought into the open. We must recall, in this connection, that Arthur was a self-abnegating man who would not have allowed personal considerations to stand in the way of achieving the common welfare.

Throughout this history, if we leave Galahad out of account, only the cuckold Arthur emerges completely unsullied in the purity of his motives and the selfless- ness of his conduct, which is what makes his final failure a tragedy on the scale of Hamlet's.

Now Agravaine and Mordred, out of petty jealousy, commit what is the ultimate crime. Agravaine, alone with his four brothers after Launcelot's healing of Sir Urre, says to them: "I marvel that we all be not ashamed both to see and to know how Sir Launcelot lieth daily and nightly by the queen, and all we know it so; and it is shamefully suffered of us all, that we all should suffer so noble a king as King Arthur is so to be shamed." He proposes to tell the King. Immediately Gawaine, fore- seeing the cataclysmic consequences, urges Agravaine to do no such thing. In this he is backed by Gaheris and Gareth; but Mordred supports Agravaine, who says: "Fall of it what fall may, I will disclose it to the king." At this point the King approaches and Gawaine, taking a hurried departure with his two like-minded brothers, exclaims: "Alas, now is this realm wholly mischieved, and the noble fellowship of the Round Table shall be disparply [scattered]."

Arthur, entering, asks what the noise is about. "My lord, said Agravaine, I shall tell you that I may keep no longer . . . that Sir Launcelot holdeth your queen, and hath done long; and we be your sister's sons, and we may suffer it no longer." So the fatal words are spoken that, once uttered, must irremediably transform the world. "The king," Malory writes, "was full loath thereto, that any noise should be upon Sir Launcelot and his queen; for the king had a deeming, but he would not hear of it, for Sir Launcelot had done so much for him and the queen so many times. . . ."

However, no longer a free man now, all he could reply was that such an accusation should not be made without proof.

Agravaine answers that, if the King will go away overnight, "then upon pain of death we shall take [Sir Launcelot] that night with the queen, and outher we shall bring him to you dead or quick." The King has no choice but to agree.

On the night of the King's absence, then, Agravaine and Mordred gather together twelve knights to surprise Launcelot in the Queen's bed-chamber. The hitherto latent factionalism of the court is revealed by the circumstance that all twelve are Scottish, which is to say that they are compatriots of the two brothers from Orkney, in opposition to the Breton Launcelot and his kin. Launcelot is duly taken in the trap by the Orkney brothers and their band, but in fighting his way out of it he succeeds in killing all of them except Sir Mordred, who escapes with a wound. From now on, however, Sir Launcelot will be at war in the cause of a patent falsehood, for he will perforce deny the accusation of adultery in order to save the Queen's life. Morally, the great age is already gone as all pretence of living up to chivalric ideals crumbles, and all parties, now governed by implacable circumstances rather than by their own wills, fight simply to save themselves.

Sir Launcelot, having slain Sir Agravaine and the twelve knights, immediately gathers together his own faction and tells what the situation is, concluding: "and for by cause I have slain this night these knights, I wot well as is Sir Agravaine Sir Gawaine's brother, and at the least twelve of his fellows, for this cause now I am sure of mortal war, for these knights were sent and ordained by King Arthur to betray me. And therefore the king will in this heat and malice judge the queen to the fire, and that may I not suffer, that she should be brent for my sake; for I will fight for the queen, that she is a true lady unto her lord."

Launcelot's dilemma is terrible but inescapable. He must do battle with many who have been his close friends and companions in the great fellowship, including King Arthur himself, and he must either kill them or allow the Queen to be burned at the stake for adultery. One is reminded of the opening of the Hindu classic, the Bhagavad-Gita , in which Arjuna pauses in horror before embarking on an internecine war that, nevertheless, he has no choice but fight:

> Arjuna stayed his chariot between the two armies. He saw in either relatives, benefactors, and friends. He saw kindred civilizations opposed, and destruction certain for one of them and perhaps for both. His limbs trembled, his purpose weakened, and instead of proclaiming battle, he spoke thus to the god Krishna, who was his charioteer: "I desire not victory nor kingdom nor pleasures. . . . Those for whose sake we desire such things—they stand opposite to us in the battle now. . . . When kindred are destroyed, the immemorial traditions perish; when traditions perish, anarchy falls on us all.

Launcelot's faction are unanimous in advising him that, as he recognizes himself, he has no choice but fight to save the Queen from the justice of the age. But "Sir Launcelot stood still, and said: My fair lords, wit you well I would be loath to do that thing that should dishonour you or my blood, and wit you well I would be

184

loath that my lady, the queen, should die a shameful death; but an it be so that ye will counsel me to rescue her, I must do much harm or I rescue her; and peradventure I shall there destroy some of my best friends, that should much repent me; and peradventure there be some, an they could well bring it about, or disobey my lord King Arthur, they would soon come to me, the which I were loathe to hurt." But the government of circumstances has now taken over.

The King, on his side, is equally distressed and helpless when Sir Mordred reports how Launcelot has been surprised in the bed-chamber of the Queen. "Alas, me sore repenteth [he says] that ever Sir Launcelot should be against me. Now I am sure the noble fellowship of the Round Table is broken for ever, for with him will many a noble knight hold; and now it is fallen so, said the king, that I may not with my worship, but the queen must suffer the death." (For "the law was such in those days," Malory reports, "that whomsoever they were, of what estate or degree, if they were found guilty of treason, there should be none other remedy but death.")

So the Queen is brought to the stake, Sir Launcelot and his faction ride to her rescue, in the affray that follows many knights of the Round Table are killed, including Gaheris and Gareth, and in the end the Queen is carried off by Launcelot to his own castle. He has now intervened to prevent justice and is an outlaw. But "many great lords and some kings sent Sir Launcelot many good knights, and many noble knights drew unto Sir Launcelot."

For Arthur the more terrible deed is not the adultery, which God himself had forgiven (and of which he himself had had a "deeming"), but its public betrayal. "Ah Agravaine, Agravaine, said the king, Jesu forgive it thy soul, for thine evil will that thou and thy brother Sir Mordred hadst unto Sir Launcelot hath caused all this sorrow."

Arthur and Launcelot are now constrained to make war against each other in opposition to their own wills. When, in a battle outside Launcelot's castle, Sir Bors downs the King, he draws his sword and says to Launcelot: "Shall I make an end of this war? and that he meant to have slain King Arthur." Launcelot replies: "I will never see that most noble king that made me knight neither slain ne shamed. And therewithal Sir Launcelot alit off his horse and took up the king and horsed him again, and said thus: My lord Arthur, for God's love stint this strife, for ye get here no worship, and I would do mine utterance, but always I forbear you, and ye nor none of yours forbeareth me. . . . Then when King Arthur was on horseback, he looked upon Sir Launcelot, and then the tears brast out of his eyen, thinking on the great courtesy that was in Sir Launcelot more than in any other man; and therewith the king rode his way, and might no longer behold him, and said: Alas, that ever this war began."

At this point, in distant Rome the greatest moral authority in the world, the vicar of Christ on earth, hearing of the fratricidal war and foreseeing that it will bring the downfall of Christian civilization, intervenes. Arthur receives a papal bull "charging him upon pain of interdicting of all England, that he take his queen Dame Guenever unto him again, and accord with Sir Launcelot."

Here is the last possible chance to save the world. One of the elements of the tragedy that marks the final part of Le Morte d'Arthur, however, is a deterioration in the characters of Launcelot and Arthur alike. Launcelot himself is faced with the ethical dilemma so common to the experience of us all (and yet so little recognized), that which arises when one inviolable principle of morality can be honored only by violating another. He can tell the truth only at the cost of betraying the Queen, and he can honor his moral obligation to the Queen only by lying. He chooses the latter and consistently denies that Guenever ever committed adultery with him.

Arthur, for his part, is a broken man now that his life's work lies in ruins, the fellowship of the Round Table forever destroyed. With his mission in life gone, without goal or purpose left, he becomes no more than the puppet of his strong-willed nephew, Sir Gawaine, who upon the death of his brothers Gaheris and Gareth (unintentionally killed by Launcelot in the mélée that attended the rescue of the Queen) has dedicated himself to avenge them by killing Launcelot. So Arthur obeys the Pope in agreeing to take Guenever back as his queen, but he unhappily gives way to Gawaine's insistence that, in spite of the Pope's order, he refuse to be reconciled with Launcelot.

Launcelot does the best that is left him to do. He returns Guenever to Arthur, and then he accepts for himself and his companions exile overseas in the land that is now France. His constant aim to the end is to minimize the disaster that has fallen on everyone through his trespass.

Arthur, on the other hand, with no purpose or direction of his own left, like a blind man simply follows the leading of Gawaine. Preparing a great expedition to follow Launcelot overseas, he leaves Gawaine's only remaining brother, Mordred, in charge of the kingdom, with Queen Guenever under his governance. This prepares the way for the fulfillment of the tragedy in terms that are the consequence of an offense committed by Arthur in his youth, albeit unwittingly, against the normative order. Here, for once, we have the element that so dominates Greek tragedy, especially in the history of Oedipus: the gods betray good men into trespasses that they could not know as such at the time, and then inflict terrible retribution upon them.

The still unwedded Arthur, before he had known that he was the son of King Uther Pendragon and Queen Igraine, had lain with their daughter Morgause, the mother of the Orkney clan, and had thereby begotten Mordred upon her. Later only did he learn from Merlin that she was his sister, and that the child of his incestuous begetting would be the agent of divine justice by destroying him and all the knights of his realm at a great battle by Salisbury. Arthur, when he appointed Mordred regent, therefore knew that he was his son as well as his nephew, and he knew of the prophecy. Now, however, he was simply obeying Gawaine, carrying out the final scenes of the drama like a sleep-walker.

Having given Sir Mordred "the rule of his land and of his wife," Arthur "passed the sea and landed upon Sir Launcelot's lands, and there he brent and wasted, through the vengeance of Sir Gawaine, all that they might overrun."

Launcelot, profoundly unwilling to fight back against the man who has been his king and against those who had so long been his fellows, sends him fair proffers of peace through the embassy of a damosel, who upon her arrival at King Arthur's camp is sadly informed by one of his knights that "my lord Arthur would love Launcelot, but Sir Gawaine will not suffer him." When the damosel presents Launcelot's suit for peace before King Arthur, "the water ran out of the king's eyen, and all the lords were full glad for to advise the king as to be accorded with Sir Launcelot, save all only Sir Gawaine, and he said: My lord mine uncle, what will ye do ? Will ye now turn again now ye are passed thus far upon this journey ? all the world will speak of your villainy. Nay, said Arthur, wit thou well, Sir Gawaine, I will do as ye advise me; and yet meseemeth, said Arthur, his fair proffers were not good to be refused." He then tells him: "I will that ye give the damosel her answer, for I may not speak to her for pity, for her proffers be so large."

So, with the momentum and inevitability of a Greek tragedy, the whole drama moves on towards its end. When Gawaine's answer reaches Launcelot, he, like Arthur, weeps, telling his knights: "I will always flee that noble king that made me knight. And when I may no further, I must needs defend me, and that will be more worship for me and us all than to compare with that noble king whom we have all served."

For half a year Arthur and Gawaine besiege Launce-lot in the fortified city of Benwick. Reluctantly, when he can no longer escape it, Launcelot twice enters into single combat with Gawaine, sparing his life both times despite Gawaine's fury at being accorded such mercy.

The turning point comes, and the final scene on the field of Salisbury is prepared, when Sir Mordred, profiting by Arthur's absence, declares himself King of England and prepares to take as his own wife Queen Guenever, who manages, however, to find refuge in the Tower of London. Arthur, Gawaine, and their host immediately lift the siege of Benwick to return across the sea and deal with Mordred.

In the fighting that accompanies their landing at Dover, opposed by Mordred and his forces, Gawaine is fatally wounded. As he lies dying in the King's arms he says: "Mine uncle King Arthur, wit you well my death day is come, and all is through mine own hastiness and wilfulness. . .; and had Sir Launcelot been with you as he was, this unhappy war had never begun; and of all this am I causer. . . ." Repenting his refusal to be reconciled with Launcelot, he calls for paper, pen, and ink and, propped up by the King, writes a note in which he beseeches Sir Launcelot to return to Arthur's realm. "Also Sir Launcelot, for all the love that ever was betwixt us, make no tarrying, but come over the sea in all haste, that thou mayst with thy noble knights rescue that noble king that made thee knight, that is my Lord Arthur; for he is full straitly bestad with a false traitor that is my half-brother, Sir Mordred. . . ."

The final battle on the field of Salisbury takes place, however, before there is time for Sir Launcelot to return. The two sides, says Malory, "fought all the long day, and never stinted till the noble knights were laid to the cold earth; and ever they fought still till it was near night, and by that time was there an hundred thousand laid dead upon the down."

Then the king looked about him, and then was he ware, of all his host and of all his good knights, were left no more on live but two knights; that one was Sir Lucan the Butler, and his brother Sir Bedivere, and they were full sore wounded. Jesu mercy, said the king, where are all my noble knights become ? Alas that ever I should see this doleful day, for now, said Arthur, I am come to mine end. But would to God that I wist where were that traitor Sir Mordred, that hath caused all this mischief. Then was King Arthur ware where Sir Mordred leaned upon his sword among a great heap of dead men. Now give me my spear, said Arthur unto Sir Lucan, for yonder I have espied the traitor that all this woe hath wrought. Sir, let him be, said Sir Lucan, for he is unhappy; and if ye pass this unhappy day ye shall be right well revenged upon him. . . . Therefore, for God's sake, my lord, leave off by this, for blessed be God ye have won the field, for here we be three on live, and with Sir Mordred is none on live; and if ye leave off now this wicked day of destiny is past. Tide me death, betide me life, saith the king, now I see him yonder alone he shall never escape mine hands, for at a better avail shall I never have him. God speed you well, said Sir Bedivere. Then the king gat his spear in both his hands, and ran toward Sir Mordred, crying: Traitor, now is thy death day come. And when Sir Mordred heard Sir Arthur, he ran until him with his sword drawn in his hand. And there King Arthur smote Sir Mordred under the shield, with a foin of his spear, through-out the body, more than a fathom. And when Sir Mordred felt that he had his death wound he thrust himself with the might that he had up to the bur of King Arthur's spear. And right so, he smote his father

Arthur, with his sword holden in both his hands, on the side of the head, that the sword pierced the helmet and the brain pan, and therewithal Sir Mordred fell stark dead to the earth; and the noble Arthur fell in a swoon to the earth, and there he swooned ofttimes.

Sir Lucan dies of his wounds, leaving only Sir Bedivere of all the King's party alive on the ground, holding the dying King in his arms.

What remains to tell is best known through the words of Malory as transmuted by Tennyson into some of the most beautiful music in the English language: how Sir Bedivere, after two false starts, threw Arthur's great sword Excalibur far out into a mere, where an arm emerged from the water, caught it, and drew it under forever; how Sir Bedivere carried Arthur on his back to the barge at the edge of the water in which three queens waited to take him away, out of this life. "Then Sir Bedivere cried: Ah my lord Arthur, what shall become of me, now ye go from me and leave me here alone among mine enemies ? Comfort thyself, said the king, and do as well as thou mayest, for in me is no trust for to trust in; for I will into the vale of Avilion to heal me of my grievous wound: and if thou hear never more of me, pray for my soul."

So he departed this life. But men said, in Malory's day, that there was written upon his tomb: HIC JACET ARTHURUS REX, QUONDAM REX QUE FUTURUS. And men said that he would come again.

Who can say that he has not in fact come again, century after century, in the persons of all those who have struggled to realize, here below, the civilizing mission that, repeatedly undertaken, repeatedly falls into disaster ? If the struggle is never won, however, neither is it finally lost. And who knows what the final end may be ?

ANTONY AND CLEOPATRA

INTRODUCTION

The three heroes presented so far, Hamlet, Odysseus, and Arthur, have in common their dedication, each in his own way, to the realization of a normative vision—its realization in defiance of the corruption that constitutes the condition of life on earth. No such dedication distinguishes the protagonists of Shakespeare's Antony and Cleopatra, even though their conduct is necessarily judged by normative standards. I have therefore resisted the temptation to find some ingenious justification for listing it as a fourth classic that illustrates my theme.

If I have allowed myself to present the other three in the pedantic context that a theme entails, I eschew all pedantry in my celebration of Antony and Cleopatra, offering it simply as a tribute of love.

There are moments, especially in the second half of this poem, that for me are unmatched in their eloquence, their poignancy, and their sheer verbal beauty. A cosmologist has written: "The effort to understand the universe is one of the very few things that lifts human life a little above the level of farce, and gives it some of the grace of tragedy."* "The grace of tragedy," as represented by Antony and Cleopatra, may alone serve as the justification for an existence that would otherwise be as sordid as it was meaningless.

---

* Steven Weinberg, The First Three Minutes: A Modern View of the Origin of the Universe, New York, 1977—the concluding sentence.

If the measure of tragedy is the nobility of its victims, Antony and Cleopatra cannot rank with Hamlet, King Lear, and Macbeth. The eponymous heroes of these three tragedies, however they actually conduct themselves, have an innate moral stature lacking in either Antony or Cleopatra. Antony arouses our sympathy by being so greatly alive and so human in his moral weakness—as Falstaff, in his own way, does too. Like Falstaff in the final scene of King Henry IV (Part Two), he is a dissolute older man put down by a young prig; and our sympathies are not where righteousness would have them. Still, Antony is not Hamlet, and the measure of his tragedy is by so much the less.

Antony and Cleopatra is a love-story, and as such it gains from the fact that the love of its protagonists is founded, not on the unfulfilled yearnings of a Romeo and Juliet, but on the constant sexual enjoyment they have of each other. Where Romeo is still a mere boy, and Juliet is only thirteen, the grizzled Antony is in his fifties and Cleopatra in her late thirties. She had borne a son to Julius Caesar years before, and has since borne several children to Antony. Their love, then, is the practiced love of a couple ripe in years, a kind of love that represents reality as the youthful dream of romantic love does not. It is like that of Malory's Launcelot and Guenever in all except the character of the hero. But Antony, too, is torn between something like duty and a tidal passion that constantly sweeps him away from it. He, too, tries and fails to free himself from the passion before disaster occurs. As for Cleopatra, she is another Guenever. She will have her knight to heel although it means the ruin of the world.

+   +   +

The wild mallards that float in loose bands on the waterways of Europe today, as on the Thames in Shakespeare's day, are usually grouped in pairs, the smaller female in the lead, the drake just behind her. When they rise in flight, she is the first to take off, and on the wing he follows her. This describes the relationship between Cleopatra and Antony, which finally brings about his downfall when she, seized by panic during the sea-battle of Actium, turns away in flight with all her ships. Then, as one of Antony's officers describes it:

> The noble ruin of her magic, Antony,
> Claps on his sea-wing, and like a doting mallard,
> Leaving the fight in height, flies after her.

From beginning to end, wherever she is, there Antony must be; wherever she goes, he is drawn after.

The empire of the world rests on the shoulders of the triumvirate composed of Mark Antony, the young Octavius Caesar, and Lepidus. Antony, the senior triumvir, and the most commanding figure, had been second only to Julius Caesar in the days of the latter's dictatorship. (We remember him in his younger days as easily the most attractive figure in Shakespeare's Julius Caesar.) Octavius Caesar, Julius's son by adoption, is embarked on a career that will invest him with the title of Augustus when he becomes the founder of the Principate. Lepidus is negligeable.

While Antony is living his extravagant life with Cleopatra in Egypt, the opponents of the triumvirate's rule are making headway against it. When, at last, this situation has become so desperate as to leave him no practicable choice but to tear himself from the scene of his pleasure and go to Rome, there to reconcile himself with "the scarce-bearded Caesar" and help restore the security of their joint rule, a soothsayer in his train urges him to return to Egypt again, saying:

> Thy demon, that thy spirit which keeps thee, is
> Noble, courageous, high, unmatchable,
> Where Caesar's is not; but near him thy angel
> Becomes a fear, as being o'erpowered; therefore

Make space enough between you. . . .
If thou dost play with him at any game
Thou art sure to lose, and, of that natural luck,
He beats thee 'gainst the odds; thy lustre thickens
When he shines by. I say again, thy spirit
Is all afraid to govern thee near him,
But he away, 'tis noble.

In an abortive attempt to make the reconciliation between the two more enduring than his Egyptian attachment will ever allow, Antony marries young Caesar's sister, Octavia, who is to Cleopatra as the image of Sacred Love to that of Profane Love in Renaissance paintings. The marriage tests his good faith and shows it wanting. To his new wife he says:

Read not my blemishes in the world's report;
I have not kept my square, but that to come
Shall all be done by the rule.

Only a moment later, however, he is saying to himself:

I will to Egypt;
And though I make this marriage for my peace,
I' the east my pleasure lies.

When the time comes, and with no evidence of compunction, he returns to his Profane Love, thereby at last giving Caesar occasion to take arms against him. What follows is Actium.

The truth is that Antony is torn, not between pleasure and moral duty, but between pleasure and the opposing demands of a political self-interest on which his survival depends. The conflict in which he finds himself is not primarily an inner conflict; and, indeed, he does not have the capacity for thoughtful introspection on which inner conflict depends. (In making his decision to leave Octavia he experiences no such struggle with conscience as Macbeth does in his decision to murder Duncan.) What he represents is a type of the eternal masculine, as Cleopatra represents a type of the eternal feminine. He is a doer, not a philosopher. We know by report that he has been a general of exemplary courage

199

and daring, enduring without complaint, when on campaign, a life of the most extreme hardship. When not on campaign, however, he likes his beds soft. He can outdrink the world and rise to drink again. He is, moreover, impulsive, not thoughtful enough even to be a schemer. Because he scorns a calculating strategy he is inevitably beaten by a Caesar who does not; and this is what gives the Soothsayer's analysis its point.

+   +   +

Just as the respective characters of Hamlet, Macbeth, and Lear change under the stress of adversity, so do the respective characters of Antony and Cleopatra as, after the defeat of Actium, the consequences close in on them. The change in Antony is a deterioration that manifests itself in an increasingly wild capriciousness. His energy bursts out in contrary directions, so that at one moment he is calling for one last "gaudy night," at the next proclaiming the mighty deeds of arms he will still execute upon the boy Caesar. His military companion of the years, Enobarbus, whose comments have salted the first half of the play, remarks to himself:

> I see still,
> A diminution in our captain's brain
> Restores his heart. When valour preys on reason
> It eats the sword it fights with.

At the end, when he has pitifully botched even his own self-destruction, all that remains of Antony is a former colossus denuded of his dignity, reduced to the stature of a child.

Cleopatra's case is the opposite. Until the last, when she is brought face-to-face with the imminent doom of her world, she is more child than queen. Charmides and Iris, her attendants, are her playmates more than they are ladies-in-waiting to a monarch. Even Antony is simply a greater playmate whom she will not relinquish to Caesar or Octavia. Despite her years, she enjoys games, doffing decorum with the ease and grace of a child in order to engage in them. Enobarbus, telling his cronies in Rome about her, says:

200

                                    I saw her once
Hop forty paces through the public street;
And having lost her breath, she spoke, and panted,
That she did make defect perfection,
And, breathless, power breathe forth.

To this he adds the classic description:

Age cannot wither her, nor custom stale
Her infinite variety; other women cloy
The appetites they feed, but she makes hungry
Where most she satisfies; for vilest things
Become themselves in her, that the holy priests
Bless her when she is riggish.

Cleopatra has not been playing the game of love
over so many years without mastering the cunning by
which men are kept on the hook. When she has to
combat the Roman thoughts that are drawing Antony
from her, she resorts to the art by which, for thousands
of years, in Egypt as in ancient Britain, aging queens
have retained their sovereignty over men's hearts.
Sending Charmian to find him, she says:

See where he is, who's with him, what he does;
I did not send you: if you find him sad,
Say I am dancing; if in mirth, report
That I am sudden sick: . . .

When Antony tells her the circumstances that compell him
to return to Rome she replies:

Nay, pray you, seek no colour for your going.
But bid farewell and go: when you sued staying
Then was the time for words; no going then:
Eternity was in our lips and eyes,
Bliss in our brows bent; none our parts so poor
But was a race of heaven; they are so still,
Or thou, the greatest soldier of the world,
Art turned the greatest liar.

Drawing herself up as a tall as she can, then, so that
her head perhaps reaches the height of his shoulder,
she adds:

I would I had thy inches; thou shouldst know
There were a heart in Egypt.

Yet go he must, leaving her pitiful.

                              O Charmian,
Where think'st thou he is now ? Stands he, or sits he ?
Or does he walk; or is he on his horse ?
O happy horse, to bear the weight of Antony !
. . . . He's speaking now,
Or murmuring 'Where's my serpent of old Nile ?'
For so he calls me.

Until the last act, however, she continues a child
companioned by children like herself. Passing the time of
Antony's absence with Charmian, she asks:

                         Did I, Charmian,
Ever love Caesar so ?

    CHARMIAN.   O ! that brave Caesar !

    CLEOPATRA.   Be choked with such another emphasis !
Say the brave Antony.

    CHARMIAN.   The valiant Caesar !

    CLEOPATRA.   By Isis, I will give thee bloody teeth,
If thou with Caesar paragon again
My man of men.

    CHARMIAN.   By your most gracious
pardon, I sing but after you.

    CLEOPATRA.   My salad days,
When I was green in judgment, cold in blood,
To say as I said then !

    There is no doubt that, over the years, Cleopatra's
feminine vanity has found its satisfaction in the greatness of the men she has conquered. It is no coincidence
that, in an earlier generation, she had ensnared the
elder Caesar (to whom she had had herself smuggled, at
the dead of night, rolled up for delivery in some rugs)

and the elder Pompey. Day-dreaming after Antony's departure, she feeds herself, as she puts it, "with most delicious poison."

> Think on me,
> That am with Phoebus' amorous pinches black,
> And wrinkled deep in time ? Broad-fronted Caesar,
> When thou wast here above the ground I was
> A morsel for a monarch, and great Pompey
> Would stand and make his eyes grow in my brow;
> With looking on his life.

There comes a moment when one wonders whether, upon the acquisition by the new Caesar of the greatness that had been Antony's, the fidelity of her love will not consist in continuing its attachment to the transferred greatness. Her cunning is in playing a game of which the object remains, for the moment, uncertain.

The fallen Antony has sent his schoolmaster in embassy to the triumphant Caesar, "an argument" (as one of Caesar's officers observes)

> that he is plucked, when hither
> He sends so poor a pinion of his wing,
> Which had superfluous kings for messengers
> Not many moons gone by.

When the schoolmaster returns with Caesar's message that Cleopatra's wishes will be honored if she will betray Antony, Antony tells her:

> To the boy Caesar send this grizzled head,
> And he will fill thy wishes to the brim
> With principalities.

She responds by a question, uttered as if to gain time, that reverberates in the mind with what it may imply: "That head, my lord ?" But Antony, in his increasing distraction, has not heard.

The same ambiguous cunning, which leaves open all possibilities, is in her reception of Thyreus, a messenger whom Caesar sends especially to tell her that:

> Caesar entreats,
> Not to consider in what case thou stand'st,
> Further than he is Caesar.

> CLEOPATRA.   Go on; right royal.

> THYREUS.   He knows that you embrace not Antony
> As you did love, but as you feared him.

> CLEOPATRA.   O !

> THYREUS.   The scars upon your honour therefore he
> Does pity, as constrained blemishes,
> Not as deserved.

> CLEOPATRA.   He is a god, and knows
> What is most right. Mine honour was not yielded,
> But conquered merely.

At the end of the interview, in which she offers her submission to Caesar, she gives Thyreus her hand to kiss, saying:

> Your Caesar's father oft,
> When he had mused of taking kingdoms in,
> Bestowed his lips on that unworthy place,
> As it rained kisses.

In the scenes that follow, Antony declines to the level of a child in a tantrum, ranting and denouncing without reason, until at last he proposes to kill Cleopatra on the grounds that she has conspired with Caesar against him. Thoroughly alarmed, she takes refuge in a monument that serves her as a fortress, sending her eunuch, Mardian, to tell Antony she is dead.

> Mardian, go tell him I have slain myself;
> Say that the last I spoke was 'Antony',
> And word it, prithee, piteously. Hence,
> Mardian, and bring me how he takes my death.

Mardian finds Antony in the company of his officer, Eros, still ranting against her. The false news of her death, however, has the desired effect. The storm of words breaks off abruptly. After a moment of silence, it is a new Antony whose voice we hear.

ANTONY.   Dead, then?

MARDIAN.   Dead.

ANTONY.   Unarm, Eros; the long day's task is done,
And we must sleep.

There follows the botched attempt at suicide, which leaves Antony dying a slow death, and so the great final hour of the play is at hand.

+   +   +

A tragedy is no greater than its victims, and I began by observing that neither Antony nor Cleopatra had moral stature. Yet in its close the tragedy of Antony and Cleopatra does, after all, rise to the highest level. This is because of the transfiguration of Cleopatra, who in the end achieves a perfect dignity, realizing in her matured self some divinity that had all along been hidden in the spoiled child. When at last the time is ripe for it; she embraces her death as the completion of a partial life made whole, now, in its conclusion. The last act is an apotheosis like no other in Shakespeare.

An echo of Cleopatra's childish voice may be heard, still, in the words she speaks as Antony, after pleading with her to remember him as he had formerly been, dies before her eyes:

Noblest of men, woo't die ?
Hast thou no care of me ? shall I abide
In this dull world, which in thy absence is
No better than a sty ? O ! see, my women, [Antony dies.
The crown o' the earth doth melt. My lord !
O ! withered is the garland of the war,
The soldier's pole is fallen; young boys and girls
Are level now with men; the odds is gone,
And there is nothing left remarkable
Beneath the visiting moon.

She has a final moment of distraction, after which she gathers herself together for the serenity that marks the closing moments of great tragedy.

> Our lamp is spent, it's out. Good sirs, take heart;
> We'll bury him; and then, what's brave, what's noble,
> Let's do it after the high Roman fashion,
> And make death proud to take us.

It remains to withhold from the young Caesar, now master of the world, the triumph he anticipates in parading her captive through the streets of Rome. First he sends one Proculeius as his messenger to dispell with soft words any suspicion she may have of this intention. To him she answers:

> If your master
> Would have a queen his beggar, you must tell him,
> That majesty, to keep decorum must
> No less beg than a kingdom: if he please
> To give me conquered Egypt for my son,
> He gives me so much of mine own as I
> Will kneel to him with thanks.

> Pray you, tell him
> I am his fortune's vassal, and I send him
> The greatness he has got.

At this moment, however, while her attention is distracted by Proculeius, other Romans, entering the monument by stealth, take her prisoner. Her reaction is immensely human and poignant. Nevertheless, in the grief and desperation of the event she loses neither her self-command nor her dignity. One of the most inspired passages in Shakespeare comes now, with the arrival of another of Caesar's lieutenants, Dolabella.

> DOLABELLA. Most noble empress, you have
> heard of me?

> CLEOPATRA. I cannot tell.

DOLABELLA.   Assuredly you know me.

CLEOPATRA.   No matter, sir, what I
                have heard or known.
You laugh when boys or women tell their dreams;
Is't not your trick ?

DOLABELLA.   I understand not, madam.

CLEOPATRA.   I dreamed there was an
                Emperor Antony:
O ! such another sleep, that I might see
But such another man.

DOLABELLA.   If it might please ye,—

CLEOPATRA.   His face was as the heavens,
                and therein stuck
A sun and moon, which kept their course, and lighted
The little O, the earth.

DOLABELLA.   Most sovereign creature,—

CLEOPATRA.   His legs bestrid the ocean;
                his reared arm
Crested the world; his voice was propertied
As all the tunéd spheres, and that to friends;
But when he meant to quail and shake the orb,
He was as rattling thunder. For his bounty,
There was no winter in't, an autumn 'twas
That grew the more by reaping; his delights
Were dolphin-like, they showed his back above
The element they lived in; in his livery
Walked crowns and crownets, realms and islands were
As plates dropped from his pocket.

DOLABELLA.   Cleopatra,—

CLEOPATRA.   Think you there was,
                or might be, such a man
As this I dreamed of ?

DOLABELLA.   Gentle madam, no.

                CLEOPATRA. You lie, up to the hearing
                                    of the gods.
        But, if there be, or ever were, one such,
        It's past the size of dreaming. . . .

It may be noted that this passage builds up from
fragmentary phrases to a pinnacle of eloquence, only to
return again, as in a musical composition, to the note on
which it opened.

                    +   +   +

        As the final scene of tragedy in Hamlet is intro-
duced by the comedy of Osric's intrusion, so the final
scene of Antony and Cleopatra is introduced by the
intrusion of the street-peddler who brings, in a basket
of figs, the asps which, by their poisoned bites, will
close the careers of Cleopatra and her former playmates,
thereby robbing Caesar of his triumph—"for his biting,"
says the peddler in recommending the asp, "is immortal;
those that do die of it do seldom or never recover."

        When he is at last gone, Cleopatra says to her
companion, Iras:

        Give me my robe, put on my crown; I have
        Immortal longings in me.

Arrayed in her majesty, then, she applies the asp to her
breast. Charmian, momentarily losing her self-control
(like Horatio at the end of Hamlet), cries out; and Cleopatra responds:

                            Peace, peace !
        Dost thou not see my baby at my breast,
        That sucks the nurse asleep ?

        The tragedy ends like Hamlet, with Caesar arriving
on the scene of death, in the role of Fortinbras, to
deliver the formal speech that the occasion demands of
him.

                    Take up her bed;
        And bear her women from the monument.

She shall be buried by her Antony:
No grave upon the earth shall clip in it
A pair so famous. High events as these
Strike those that make them; and their story is
No less in pity than his glory which
Brought them to be lamented. Our army shall,
In solemn show, attend this funeral,
And then to Rome. Come, Dolabella, see
High order in this great solemnity.

[As in Hamlet, the soldiers bear away the dead bodies,
while a dead march is heard.]

+   +   +

The greatest works of art are not necessarily the
least defective, and the defects of Antony and Cleopatra
need no searching. There are, as well, grounds that I
have already given for not ranking it with the greatest
tragedies. However, as the poem that it is, it has a
distinction by which it stands alone. The combination of
beauty and eloquence in its language is unmatched, even
by Shakespeare himself, in any other work.

The eloquence is that of hyperbole, and in this
alone it is unique. Metaphoric images that should be
unconvincing in their exaggeration, but are not, lift the
level of character and action to the cosmic plane, so that
boundless space seems hardly sufficient for a stage.
Antony, telling Cleopatra that he will not heed the call
to Rome, says:

Let Rome in Tiber melt, and the wide arch
Of the ranged empire fall ! Here is my space.

But he finds that he cannot limit his greatness spatially,
for he is "the triple pillar of the world." Because the
whole Mediterranean and its shores—Italy and Greece,
Parthia and Africa—require his immense presence, the
scene of his life cannot be circumscribed by the walls of
Alexandria. The life of the play itself breathes the wide
universe. In such a setting the hyperbole is not disproportionate. Upon the local scene of an ordinary play
it would have been enough that Antony, who is reduced

to sending messages of state by a schoolmaster, had once had kings for messengers. Here the very scale requires that he should once have had "superfluous kings" for messengers.

The inadequacy of Lepidus is such only against the background of Pythagorean space, which Antony and Caesar, each in his own way, are able to fill—until, at last, Antony is reduced to the proportions of any man, leaving Caesar to inaugurate the Augustan Age in which he fills it all. The servant in Pompey's galley, playing the role of the first grave-digger in Hamlet, sums up Lepidus when, in gossip with a fellow servant, he refers to him as being "called into a huge sphere," but not being "seen to move in't." As much could not have been said of Antony before his fall.

Only the world of natural phenomena can supply metaphoric images adequate to the size of the scene and its protagonists. Breathtaking as they are, however, they would still fall of their own weight if not upborne by the music of the language. All poetry is not music, and, of such as is, all is not the same kind of music. There is small music and large music. When one reads other plays of Shakespeare too, one must hear the language, not see it only. In The Merchant of Venice it has the movement of music at an Italian Renaissance court; in As You Like It and The Winter's Tale the music is half pastoral, half courtly; in Love's Labours Lost it is a minuet. The language of Antony and Cleopatra, however, is Pythagorean, uttering the music of the spheres.

Nothing in all literature equals Cleopatra's description of Antony, already cited in another context but endlessly worth repeating:

> His legs bestrid the ocean; his reared arm
> Crested the world; his voice was propertied
> As all the tunéd spheres, and that to friends;
> But when he meant to quail and shake the orb,
> He was as rattling thunder. For his bounty,
> There was no winter in't, an autumn 'twas
> That grew the more by reaping; his delights

Were dolphin-like, they showed his back above
The element they lived in; in his livery
Walked crowns and crownets, realms and islands were
As plates dropped from his pocket.

In all literature is there a simile more eloquent than that of Antony's "dolphin-like" delights, which "showed his back above the element they lived in" ? It is both visual and musical, for among the images of nature there are few so musical as that of dolphins looping in rhythmic counterpoint to the rhythm of the waves. And by a prodigy of delicate evocation, the movement described goes beyond that of the dolphins rising and falling in their arcs.

Again, there are the echoes that represent another form of rhythm in music. Antony, when he has at last declined to the bottom of his fortunes and sees that the only dignity left him is that of death, says to Eros:

Unarm, Eros; the long day's task is done,
And we must sleep.

A few scenes further on, when Cleopatra has reached the height of her self-realization but the nadir of her own fortunes, Iras says to her:

Finish, good lady; the bright day is done,
And we are for the dark.

It is a peculiarity of Shakespeare's genius that each of his characters speaks in the language of his own individuality. Each has his own eloquence, or no eloquence at all where it would be out of character. Octavia, as Enobarbus observes, "is of a holy, cold, and still conversation." Enobarbus, himself, has an eloquent and humorous bluntness appropriate to a soldier, except in his description of Cleopatra, when the inspiration of his subject lifts him momentarily to a lyric plane. The language of the young Pompey, the mediocre son of a great father, is characteristically bumpy and short-winded, issuing in abrupt phrases without grace:

I shall do well:

The people love me, and the sea is mine;
My powers are crescent, and my auguring hope
Says it will come to the full. Mark Antony
In Egypt sits at dinner, and will make
No wars without doors; Caesar gets money where
He loses hearts; Lepidus flatters both,
Of both is flattered; but he neither loves,
Nor either cares for him.

The language of Cleopatra, by contrast, represents the ineffable grace that she never loses, even after she has hopped forty paces through the public street; and in the end it rises to the sublimity I have already cited. When word comes to Antony that his first wife has died, she makes even bitterness graceful, telling him:

I prithee, turn aside and weep for her,
Then bid adieu to me, and say the tears
Belong to Egypt.

Humbled after Antony's death, she says of herself to Iras, who has just addressed her as "Royal Egypt ! Empress !":

No more, but e'en a woman, and commanded
By such poor passion as the maid that milks
And does the meanest chores. It were for me
To throw my sceptre at the injurious gods;
To tell them that this world did equal theirs
Till they had stolen our jewel.

When, at her one interview with the victorious Caesar, a disloyal servitor betrays her to Caesar by betraying a betrayal she herself had intended, she says to the servitor:

Prithee, go hence;
Or I shall show the cinders of my spirits
Through the ashes of my chance.

And at the end she manifests, over and above the grace she has always had, a new dignity not inferior to that of Shakespeare's Imogen or Portia. Imogen and Portia are what they have always been. But the Cleopatra of the death scene is as much as they are, and more by the addition of what she has been: what Antony had called "this great Fairy," the serpent of old Nile, the playmate of princes upon whom she conferred alike her delicacy, her grace, and her splendor. She is the greatest of Shakespeare's women. And so, in the end, <u>Antony and Cleopatra</u> proves to be one of the great tragedies after all.